someday i'll be somebody

someday i'll be somebody

BY MICKEY JORDAN

Foreword by Rosalind Rinker

FORUM HOUSE/Publishers

Atlanta

Printed in the United States of America.

Library of Congress catalog card number: 72-97822
ISBN: 0-913618-09-8

To my husband, O. H. Jordan, Jr.,
whose love and faith
have sustained me in my continual struggles
toward a better tomorrow.

AUTHOR'S NOTE

This is a true story. However, some of the names, places, and circumstances have been disguised to protect the privacy of those involved.

table of contents

foreword

Nothing could make me happier than to write the foreword to Mickey Jordan's first book. In our friendship through the years, I have watched her grow and mature as God's child. Very early she came to an understanding that all the painful experiences of her childhood could be turned into something beautiful.

In the reading of this book, which tells of these and many other experiences, you will find yourself more than once identifying with Mickey. For in essence, all of our hearts are longing for someone to know us as we are, and to become the person we know we really are.

In this story, you will find your belief in God's love for you strengthened again and again. God laid his hand upon Mickey even before she knew of his loving care. How exciting that now she can put her story on paper and know that it has been wrought out of the heartaches and tears of her life as a piece of rare art is wrought from shapeless metal. This has happened because God loves her with an eternal, never-changing love. Just as he loves you — and me.

ROSALIND RINKER

"i'm back, hollywood! i've come back!"

The DC-3 dropped through the clouds. There below us was the ocean, and over there, Los Angeles! We banked and descended rapidly.

Thank you, dear God, for bringing me here at last. Only you could take a girl born in a Georgia cotton patch and make her somebody. When I think how I worked in the fields from the time I was five until I was grown — how I was so tacky my schoolmates ridiculed me — I can't believe this is happening. But you promised you'd let me be somebody someday, Lord, and I thank you for giving me this chance.

The engines roared with a new burst of power. The plane shuddered, then shot ahead. We bounced as the runway came up to meet us.

Fearing we would flip over, I braced my left arm against the seat in front of me. I must have communicated my fear to the sergeant sitting next to me. He grinned and said, "That was almost a three-point landing. You ought to land with some of the hot pilots I have to fly with!"

Our eyes, as if synchronized, moved down to see my right hand clutching his left wrist. I let go and we both laughed.

"I'm sorry," I said. "I was just plain scared. I admit I've never been on one of these contraptions before. The airlines have somehow never gotten around to landing at Persimmon Grove or Henry Springs, Georgia."

I liked this good-looking, good-natured redhead. I felt a kinship with him. He was in uniform; my husband was in uniform. He was from the farm (Minnesota); I was from the farm. We spoke the same language, although with different accents.

As we taxied up to the terminal building, Red offered to share a cab with me. I was tempted to accept. Instead, I told him I was being met by an uncle. He must have known there was no uncle, for he hung back while other passengers deplaned. I kept getting my things together, combing my hair, and applying new lipstick. I said goodby and lotsa luck and went to the restroom. When I returned, he was still there. My irritation showed and he picked up his B-4 bag, saluted, and left.

The dream of a lifetime was about to be fulfilled, and I wanted to savor the moment alone. As I walked out onto the ramp, I pictured myself extending my arms to a band of well-wishers and calling out, "I'm back, Hollywood! I've come back!"

I couldn't have waved if I had tried. My arms were burdened with an overnight case, a garment bag, and two hatboxes whose brand names were far more elegant than the hats inside. And there was nobody to see me off the plane except an attendant who gave me a perfunctory, "Hope you had a pleasant flight, ma'am."

As my feet touched the pavement, my thoughts came down to earth. I acknowledged inwardly that my self-confidence was self-deception. I was alone in a strange place, I felt terribly lonesome, and I was afraid. My first visit to Hollywood had ended miserably, and so might this one. I wanted the reassurance of seeing somebody I knew. I glanced around for the sergeant but didn't see him.

I claimed my footlocker and suitcase and, with the help of a skycap, got my things into a taxi.

"Where to, miss?" the driver inquired.

He was fiftyish, a solid-citizen type. I felt I could trust him.

"I hope you can help me. I need a small room in a hotel – something nice but inexpensive."

"If you want something downtown, I'd recommend the Gold Coast."

"That'll be fine, thanks."

I feared that Hollywood itself would be too expensive. Barney Dean had recommended the Biltmore. Well, I just wouldn't tell him where I was staying. Barney, whom I had met in the home of my favorite cousin, Bernice, was an associate of Bob Hope's. Barney was my key to Hollywood. I fished around in my purse for the slip of paper with his phone number on it and was relieved to find it.

"In Hollywood," Barney had said, "it isn't *what* you know, but *who* you know. You come out and I'll ask Bob to help you get started."

As the taxi pulled away from the curb, I spotted Red and almost told the driver to stop, but didn't. I was in California for one purpose and one purpose only. I waved to Red and he gave me a shrug and a smile.

"You on vacation, miss?" The driver's question had an empty ring. He knew – and I knew that he knew.

"No, I'm out here for a career in motion pictures."

"I see."

There was a conspicuous silence. Then he said, "We get so many of them out here. Thousands. I hear that only one in a hundred lands a studio job, and the majority of these so-called lucky ones draw a starvation wage. Most of the also-rans wind up working in dime stores, slinging hash, and such. Or they go back home crushed in spirit and broke – most of them even have to wire home for money to buy their ticket. The tales that some of them tell eat my heart out. The papers are full of rapes, paternity suits, and suicide. God only knows why they keep coming."

By "they," he meant me, only he was too polite to say so.

Well, I wasn't just one more of those *theys*. He'd see. The whole world would see!

"I have an introduction to Bob Hope," I said confidently. "You do? That's good," he said, brightening. "Now there's a great comic. I hate he switched to movies 'cause I listened to him on the radio all the time. He made a good movie with Paulette Goddard just before the war – *The Cat and the Canary*. They were in this spooky old mansion and the heroine had to survive until the next morning to inherit a fortune. All night, a monster was killing off her relatives. Bob really did a great job at faking nervousness."

"He's making *Monsieur Beaucaire* now for Paramount, playing the barber," I interjected.

"But you know," the cabbie reflected, "even the stars don't have it easy. The greatest of them all – Gable – I picked him up one afternoon – in '32, I believe. His day had started at five and now he was going to another studio he'd been loaned to. He didn't know anything about this role he was assigned until he read it in the papers. He said to me, 'I'm paid *not* to think.' I said to him, 'Mr. Gable, it looks like you and me both just go wherever they send us.' And he said to me, 'Why don't you and me both just quit?' "

"Oh, that's nonsense," I said. "I've read all that stuff in the movie magazines and I don't believe a word of it. For example, Bette Davis saying that the film moguls want to *create* personalities, not be *challenged* by them. Why, Clark Gable and Bette Davis would act for a dime a day. They can't live without acting. That's the way we are. Gable was just feeling guilty because he was at the top of the stack and there were thousands of dead bodies lying around.

"The stars like to have everyone noticing whether they eat their peas with a knife or a fork, but they can't afford to admit it for fear their fans might turn on them – so they complain about hard work. Well, I don't mind hard work. I've picked cotton from daylight to dark, and I know it can't be *that* bad out here. Let the stars quit if they feel that way.

I'll work day and night. I'll go from studio to studio if they want me to," I ended grandly as we arrived at the hotel. The driver came around and opened my door. "You know," he said, "you might just make it. You'd make a good one of them Carmen Miranda spitfires. Course, they'd have to do something about your Southern accent."

"Thanks," I said, "but I'm very proud of my Southern accent."

I checked in at the hotel desk, and a bellhop took my luggage.

Although I had been on the stage since age ten, when I won the "Queen of the Charleston" crown at the Greer County Fiddlers' Convention, and although I had been in beauty pageants, the way the bellhop was mentally undressing me in the elevator completely unnerved me. He was strikingly handsome, with a Robert Taylor face, Ronald Colman hair, Cary Grant eyes, and Franchot Tone *savoir-faire*. We got off the elevator and I followed him down the dimly lit corridor to my room. He ushered me in with a grand gesture. The room was clean and comfortable-looking, if a bit worn.

He pointed out the shared bath down the hall, opened my window for me, and answered several questions. I handed him a fifty-cent piece, and his manner suggested that he thought he was doing *me* a favor by accepting it.

"It's a pleasure to serve you, Miss —."

"*Mrs.* Mickey Jordan."

"I'm Rocky Howard. If there's anything you need, just call the bell captain's desk and ask for me."

"Thanks, I'll remember."

"Your first trip out?"

"No, I was here in '37."

"Trying to break into the movies then, too?"

I resented his presumptuousness but merely answered yes.

"What happened?"

"Oh, it's a long story. I was only nineteen then. . . . But I don't want to talk about it."

"The reason I asked, I once gave the flicks a whirl. I was getting some small parts. That was in '32. In '33, in January, Paramount and RKO went into receivership. All the studios were in a bad way. Funny, but do you know who rescued Paramount? Mae West!"

"Mae West? I didn't remember that."

"I wouldn't have guessed you were old enough to remember the Depression."

"Does a person ever forget going to bed hungry?"

"I'd like to think the Depression ruined my chances," he said, "but I know that isn't really true. My wife divorced me. I really don't blame her. I guess you'd say I abandoned her when I came out here. Anyhow, I started drinking too much."

My conscience gave me a twinge.

"But you were trying to do something *good* for her! I mean, you wanted to get established before you sent for her, didn't you?"

He didn't answer.

"Well," I said, "now that I've heard your life story, I'd better get unpacked."

"I wish you luck," he said. "You've got the looks and the personality – if somebody will only give you a chance."

"They will. I'm going to be introduced to Bob Hope tomorrow."

"Say, that's great. But remember, girls stream in and out of these hotels by the thousands. Some chicks are sharp, some unsuspecting. All I can say is, be sure what you want and don't pay too high a price. Some guys out here dispose of starlets like they'd flick a used razor blade into the waste basket."

"Now, look, Rocky whatever-your-name-is, aren't you being melodramatic? I've only been in town two hours and already I've received two lectures on keeping my chin and my guard up. I can look after myself. I'm a big girl now."

"Sure you are," he said with a head-to-toes sweep of the eyes. "Just one more question. Y'all from Miss'sippi, Alabamy, or Geor-gie?"

I hated "hush-my-mouth" imitations, but his smile kept the put-on from being offensive. "Georgia. At-lan-ta." He couldn't fault *that* diction!

"You all do say that cute-like. Well, so long. See you later."

"So long, and thanks."

I undressed, put on my negligee, plopped down on the bed, and called Paramount Studios.

"Paramount Studios."

"Hello. This is Mrs. Jordan — Mickey Jordan from Atlanta, Georgia. May I please speak to Mr. Barney Dean?"

"I'm sorry, Mrs. Jordan, but Mr. Dean is out of the city."

My heart sank. I knew I should have written or called to let Barney know when I was arriving. "Can you tell me when he'll return?"

"His plane's due just about now. He may call the office before five, but I don't think you should count on it. May I take a message?"

I gave her my number. Within ten minutes, Barney called.

"Mickey! Good to hear your voice. Welcome to the City of Bright Lights."

"Oh, Barney, I was so afraid you wouldn't remember me."

"Not remember you? Listen, sweetheart, it's my business to remember the pretty girls I meet."

"Barney, do you think Mr. Hope is still interested in giving me a screen test like you said?"

"Sure. I've told him all about you. Can you come out to Paramount in the morning? Are you staying at the Biltmore?"

"No, I've got a temporary place right now."

"Good. Well, how about meeting me at the studio at nine sharp? Ask the man on the gate to call and I'll pick you up. We'll have breakfast in the commissary, where you can see some of our big names. Then we'll tour the lot. We'll catch Bob during his noon break, okay?"

"That'll be swell. Thanks, Barney. Bye."

"Bye. See you tomorrow."

See you tomorrow! Yes, tomorrows do come!

I waltzed around the room, then flopped on the bed and let my arms and legs hang loose. It was the first time I had relaxed in three days.

Suddenly, my anxiety returned. My big moment had come, but would I measure up? I went over to the full-length mirror and inspected my silhouette, throwing back my shoulders while pulling in my tummy. What would they want in a screen test? I gathered up my negligee to expose more leg and tossed my head, causing my long, black hair to swirl through the air.

This is stupid, I said to myself. My alter ego replied, "It may be stupid, but it's Hollywood!"

I read a movie magazine, listened to the radio, gazed out my window. I was tired from the trip but too excited to nap. I was developing "cabin fever," so I decided to go downstairs for a hamburger and a cup of coffee. I would have to watch my expenses, because I only had thirty-seven dollars left. To finance the trip, I had cashed my first Army allotment check from Ollie, hocked my engagement and wedding rings, and borrowed twenty dollars. The fact that I had bought a one-way plane ticket made me feel insecure. Well, what counted was I was in Hollywood and had good contacts.

Entering the coffee shop, I noticed Rocky at a table in the back with two blousy painted dolls and a George-Raft-type guy. They were tossing down drinks. The girls giggled and couldn't keep their hands off the two men. Once, when the others weren't looking, Rocky gave me a little wave, which I half-heartedly acknowledged. I ate and went back to my room.

Later, having tired of the radio, I opened the Gideons' Bible to the book of Luke. I read to where Jesus' family journeyed to Jerusalem when he was twelve. On the way home they missed him and went back to find him conversing with the teachers in the synagogue. Jesus told his parents that they might have known he'd be there; nevertheless, he went home with them and was obedient to them. "And Mary treasured these things in her heart," it said.

Jesus had a loving, understanding family. I wanted so much for my own family to be that way. There were memories I treasured in my heart, but right now my heart was filled with loneliness and guilt — so much guilt that I reached over and turned the photograph of my husband and my babies face down on the dresser. Then, ashamed, I picked up the picture and looked into their faces — Ollie; Gayle, who was five; and Sandra, only three. Oh, how I wanted to learn to love Ollie the way he needed to be loved, and I wanted Ollie to be able to love me the way I needed to be loved. During our last few days together, three months earlier, we seemed to have a real spark between us. Was it real? Was I remembering — or fantasizing?

I'll always remember the day that Ollie came home with the news. November 15, 1944. It was only ten o'clock, too early for lunch. He just stood in the doorway, not saying a thing.

"Ollie, are you sick?"

He didn't reply.

I put my arms around his waist. "Ollie," I said, "are you still hurt because I keep begging you to let me go back to Hollywood for just one more chance?"

I had already made up my mind that I was going, whether Ollie gave his permission or not. After trying a dozen approaches with no success, I no longer intended to ask. I would just go and leave him a note. I would accept the consequences, whatever they were. If I succeeded in launching a movie career, Ollie would be proud. And if I failed, he just might be glad to have me home again.

"It isn't that," Ollie said. "I know you wouldn't really leave us for that crazy dream of yours. No, it isn't that. I've been drafted!"

Ollie — drafted? Because we had two children, we figured he wouldn't be called.

"When do you have to report?"

"December first."

Twin shock waves raced over my brain. I hated to see Ollie go, for his own sake as much as anything else. You wouldn't wish the Army off on *anybody*. I would miss him — certainly I didn't relish the idea of managing things alone. But the calculating part of my mind celebrated: "Whoopee, here's your chance. Once Ollie is away, you can go to Hollywood. What Ollie doesn't know won't hurt him." If ever I needed to use my acting talent, it was then. I bit my lower lip to assure a pained countenance.

Despite the cloud hanging over us, the next two weeks were joyous. Ollie took a good bit of time from his work — time which we spent together doing as we pleased.

The days flew and soon Ollie was gone. The outside chance that he would get a three-day pass at Christmas vanished with the heavy losses of American troops in Germany. March came and Ollie had only two more weeks of basic training, to be followed by a furlough. I knew I had to make my move right away.

When I told Mother my intention, she wouldn't even discuss it. I called Bernice and begged her influence. Bernice told Mother I had to get Hollywood out of my system once and for all, and now was the best time. Eventually Mother yielded and agreed to keep Gayle and Sandra.

So, here we were, Ollie stuck in a basic-training hellhole and me all the way across the continent chasing that "crazy dream." Would Ollie ever forgive me? He was bound to learn about my trip. And my little girls. How could they understand why I had deserted them?

Feelings of guilt and loneliness were beginning to smother me. I slipped on my robe and walked down the hall toward the bathroom. From the room next to the bathroom came giggling and loud talk. One of the voices was Rocky's.

As I came out into the hall again, the door of the partying room opened and Rocky staggered into the hall. When he saw me he called out, "Well, here'sh our li'l Zorsha peash." He stumbled over, put his arm around my neck, and said,

"You're zush in time. We're having a li'l party and Marie went to sleep on me."

Inside the room, I could see Marie in one bed. On the other bed, scantily clad, was the second woman and the other man. "C'mon and have a drink, Peash," Rocky said, pulling me toward the room.

"No, Rocky, I can't. I've got to get up early tomorrow, remember? I've got to go to the studio and see Mr. Hope." "Bob Hope," he said. "You're going to see Bob Hope, but ol' Rocky isn't good enough for you." His grip cut into my arm. I tried to jerk away. "Hey, Nick," Rocky called, "come out here and help me bring this damn Zorsha peash to our party."

Nick extricated himself and came in my direction. I screamed. A nearby door popped open and a woman's head appeared just in time to see them drag me into the room. "Help!" I cried. "Somebody, please help me!"

"Rocky, let her go or we're in bad trouble," Nick said. "No," Rocky grumbled. "I insish she come to our party." Nick closed the door and stood guard. Rocky tugged me over to the dresser, then let go. "Whash you need, Peash, is a drink," he said. He did a miserable job trying to make a connection between the stream of whiskey issuing from the bottle and the glass he held.

Meanwhile, Painted Doll No. 2, who had been silently contemplating the scene, beckoned to Nick. "C'mon back over here, Nicky. Let ol' Rocky look after *her*. *You* look after *me*."

There was a sharp rap on the door. "Open up. It's the house detective."

Nick unbolted the door, which flew open. A man, his hand on a pistol in his belt, rushed in, followed by another man. The first, apparently the house detective, glared at Rocky and said, "Rocky, you just can't leave 'em alone, can you?" And to me, "You the one who screamed?"

"Yes." And I started bawling.

"I'm Mr. Anderson, the night manager," the other man said. "I'm terribly sorry about this incident. Do you want to prefer charges?"

I looked at Rocky, who was clinging to the lavatory and looking at me bleakly.

"No, I guess not," I sobbed.

"Well, you can rest assured he's fired. He won't bother you again. Dave, get all of them out of here."

The detective lifted Marie's head by her long hair and began slapping her. "Marie," he said sternly, "get up, get your clothes on, and get out!" Meanwhile, Painted Doll No. 2 had put on her dress and, shoes in hand, quietly departed.

"C'mon, you two," the detective said to Rocky and Nick. "John, I'll be back for her," he said, indicating Marie.

Again, the manager began apologizing.

"Don't try to talk to me," I said. "All I want is to get out of this terrible hotel."

"But ma'am, you don't want to try to find another place in the middle of the night, do you? Wouldn't you prefer to wait until morning?"

"Oh, I don't know what to do," I sobbed.

Trying to comfort me, he said, "We'll move you down to the second floor. A nice room with adjoining bath."

"But that sounds expensive."

"It won't cost you one red cent more," he assured me. "And tomorrow if you decide you don't want to move again, you can stay right here."

I was still trembling. He asked if I wanted him to call the house doctor. I shook my head.

The manager got my things moved. When I told him I had to get some sleep because I had an appointment in Hollywood at nine, he said he would have me delivered to Paramount in the hotel's courtesy car.

I said goodnight and sat on the edge of my bed. Filling my window was the upper structure and steeple of a beautiful stone church across the street. I recalled the first time I had been in church. An innocent child wearing worn, soiled clothes, I had gone down the aisle and offered myself to Christ. God's hand was in my life. God loved me, wanted me to be somebody. Hadn't he sent Barney Dean to me? Hadn't he (granted, some aspects were hard to understand) arranged for Ollie to go away in the service? Hadn't God persuaded Mother to care for my babies? Still, people were saying things to discourage me. And now *this* episode. I would look awful in the morning. Was God trying to tell me something?

I turned off the bedside lamp. A spotlight illuminated the church steeple, and the reflection gave my room a soft glow.

Dear God, you know that deep in my heart I want to do your will, but I can't help it if you gave me such a strong will of my own. My ambition is like red hot coals within me. You encouraged me to come out here. You promised to help me. Well, here I am, and I need your help terribly.

I admit I'm proud and selfish; but honest, I'm not doing this for myself alone. I want to give Ollie, my babies, and my mother and daddy things I can't give them now. I want them to be proud of me. And I want to be successful for your sake, too, so when I witness, people will listen.

Forgive my stupid mistakes. I've made so many. Take charge of my life once again. Tell me what you want me to do and I'll do it. If I was mistaken about your wanting me to come out here, say so and I'll pack and leave. Sure, it would break my heart, but I'd do it. But I pray it's your will for me to impress Mr. Hope and get a chance to prove myself. I want to do great things in your name.

Lord, be with Ollie. Please make him understand. Watch over Mother and my babies, too. And, Lord, please make Ollie and me love each other so much we will never again let each other go.

I clutched my family's picture to my breast. I felt that God was with me in that room so far from home. I believed that he did, indeed, want me to be somebody.

My trouble was, it soon became apparent, that I didn't know what sort of somebody God wanted me to be.

2

"let's call her 'pretty mickey'"

How many times my mother has told me, "Mickey, it's a wonder you weren't born in the middle of a cotton patch."

On the day preceding the night when I was born, Mother got up at 4 a.m., cooked breakfast, milked a cow, and put a tub of clothes on the line. Then she toted Earl, age two, to the field. She set him down under a tree at one end of the patch, gave him a syrup can and a big wooden spoon to play with, and began helping Daddy plant cotton.

Mother worked her way down one long row and back up the next. Each trip, she stopped and played with Earl a minute, then moved on to plant two more rows.

At noon, Mother took Earl back to the house, fixed dinner, and brought it and Earl back to the field. After Daddy ate, he took off his shoes and let the galluses of his overalls slip off his shoulders. With his battered hat over his eyes, he lay on his back chewing on a blade of grass and resting. Ten minutes later, he and Mother went back to work.

Mother worked the rest of the afternoon, then went home and cooked supper. When Daddy came, she helped him with the chores.

At midnight, Mother began having labor pains. She woke Daddy. "Wade," she said softly, "it may be a while yet, but I'd feel more comfortable to have Nar Sis here."

Nar Sis (her name was Narcissus, most likely) was a frail old black woman who lived alone in a little shack half a mile down the road from my parents' house. She was our nearest neighbor. We lived four miles off the main road, and it was six miles to the crossroads settlement of Persimmon Grove. From Persimmon Grove to town and the nearest doctor was four additional miles. No wonder, then, that white and black alike depended on Nar Sis, the midwife. And we Sauls were among her best clients.

Daddy hitched his mule to the wagon and drove to Nar Sis's. Born with club feet, she hobbled around getting everything into her "stork satchel." Then Daddy boosted her into the wagon and drove home.

The old woman tottered into the house, put down her satchel, placed her open hand on Mother's abdomen, looked into her face, and pronounced: "Mr. Wade, you please fetch me mo' water. It ain't gonna be but twenty-fo' minutes." In her prognostications, Nar Sis always employed specific timing; it gave her already superb reputation an extra dimension of expertise.

Mother already had a kettle of water simmering in the fireplace. Daddy brought a bucket of water from the well, tossed a couple of logs on the fire, and went out on the front porch. He didn't want to be in a house where childbirth was taking place. Birthing and midwifery were "women's business."

Whether the lapsed time was precisely twenty-four minutes or not, I don't know, but at 2 a.m. I made my noisy entrance into the world. Nar Sis went to the front door and announced, "Lawsa mercy, Mr. Wade, you done got yo'self a baby girl."

Daddy came in, viewed me without comment, gave my mother a peck on the cheek, and took a seat in his rocking chair (the only chair in the house) in front of the fireplace. Soon he was asleep.

Our first visitor the next day was Mother's sister Mary, who happened to be visiting Papa and Mama Leslie. As usual, she was fashionably dressed – on this occasion in purple and lavender from head to foot. High-spirited Aunt Mary lived in Atlanta, where she had a job. Compared to us, she seemed rich.

Aunt Mary marched over, pulled back the covers, and surveyed my big eyes, tiny body, dark complexion, and still darker hair.

"Sister," she said, "have you named her?"

"Yes, Mary. Her name is Leslie – Ernestine Leslie Sauls."

"Papa'll be proud you named her Leslie for him, Sister, but I've got a better name. Let's call her 'Pretty Mickey.' "

"*Mickey*?" my father repeated incredulously. "I'd say Mickey is a heck of a girl's name. And '*Pretty* Mickey'? Mary, you must be blind as a bat."

Aunt Mary explained she had heard a new song called "Pretty Mickey" on the radio and had bought the sheet music. She said I would grow up to be like the cover girl – a dark-eyed beauty with black tresses falling over her shoulders.

So, although the name on my birth certificate is Ernestine Leslie, I've always been "Mickey."

My father took a dim view of females. He resented Aunt Mary's citified ways and liberated life-style. "Mary," he'd say, "if the Lord intended for women to talk politics, he'd have shown 'em how to spit and whittle." As to his new child, he'd rather have had another son – a son who would grow up and help him with the heavy work.

Mother fretted because I was so "peak-ed." She also was dismayed by my large eyes, which seemed to grow larger, and my thick, black hair, which grew thicker and darker. I was a year old before she conceded that I would probably turn out all right; even then, she screened me from public view whenever she could. I have my own vague recollection that while I was a little girl, Daddy didn't want me and Mother was ashamed of me.

In addition to Aunt Mary, however, there was someone who never doubted my value or my potential. That person was Papa Leslie, my grandfather and my mother's father. Papa Leslie lived between us and Persimmon Grove. Although he never did call me "*Pretty* Mickey," he did think me pretty. And sweet. He called me "Baby." Until I was five, I was a liability to my parents, whereas Earl was an asset. He could tote water to the field, help strew guano, pick potato bugs off the vines, and bring in stovewood. Because of my uselessness, I spent days and even weeks with Papa Leslie. Although Mama Leslie loved me and cared for me, too, I always spoke of going to *Papa* Leslie's. I spent most of my waking hours traipsing behind him. In retrospect, it seems strange that an old man would want the responsibility for minding a baby girl – but, then, the relationship between Papa Leslie and me wasn't an ordinary relationship. It was something very special.

When I was five, we moved three miles down the road – three miles farther from Papa Leslie. I went to his house less often. I could now do light chores and look after my little sisters, Mary and Julia. (Bobbie, Roy Russell, and Angel would follow in quick succession.) I was proud when Mother said, "This is my big girl. I don't know what I would do without Mickey!" And I was pleased when, on occasion, my father (who rarely spoke in affectionate terms) called me "Mick."

My father was a tenant farmer – a sharecropper. The boss man owned the land, bought the seed and fertilizer, and advanced a very little bit of money for whatever foodstuffs and other items proved necessary for our existence. When Daddy hauled cotton to the gin, half the proceeds went to the boss man. In a good year (when it wasn't too wet or too dry and the boll weevil didn't ruin us), Daddy might produce two or three bales of cotton, each of which would bring maybe sixty dollars. When accounts were settled, there might be thirty or forty dollars left for us to live on the next twelve months. In bad years, there would be a deficit to be carried into the next year. We had a garden, of course, and Mother canned produce for the winter. Some years we had a hog to butcher at first freeze; we kept a cow, and we raised chickens. So, we somehow managed to keep body and soul together — although keeping my soul intact was the greater task.

One of my earliest impressions is going to the gin, which was my favorite activity next to visiting Papa Leslie. We stored our cotton on the porch and in the smokehouse, which was empty that time of year. When there was enough for a bale, we loaded it into the wagon, on which side-bodies had been installed. The cotton would be so high that we kids had to tunnel under it to avoid low-hanging tree limbs. At the gin, there would be other kids to play with while Daddy waited in line. Then, when our wagon moved to the front of the procession, I would marvel at the way the chute sucked up the fleecy cargo.

With the proceeds of the cotton in hand, Daddy would first go to a store or two where he had accounts (often the boss man owned the store) and settle up. Then, in the general store, he would buy some soda crackers out of the barrel, a pound of hoop cheese, a couple of cans of sardines, and, for each of us, a bottle of soda pop. We ate this repast on wrapping paper spread out over the store counter. After lunch, if it was a good year, Daddy would let each of us kids choose a cookie from a nest of glass-doored cookie boxes. Later, Mother would take us to the dry goods store, where we would each get material for a new dress or shirt — and, if the year was good and our need dire, a pair of overalls or a pair of shoes. However, we sometimes went all, or most, of the winter without shoes.

I've heard contemporaries say that although as children they lived hard lives, they didn't recognize then how hard it was. I knew my life was hard. I hated it.

My daddy was stern. I couldn't understand how he could be so hard. Now I see him as a product of his own early environment, which was as harsh as ours. Daddy was one of fifteen children. He didn't have either the facility or the time to be demonstrably affectionate.

As I grew into school age, my burdens increased. At four in the morning, Daddy rang the big "dinner" bell, fastened atop a post in the backyard. On cold mornings, death seemed a welcome alternative to getting up, but I didn't tarry when Daddy rang that bell! If I did, he would come in with a razor strap and whack my bottom until I got out the back door. We worked at appointed chores, then came in to eat poorman's thickening gravy and a biscuit. A second biscuit I sopped in sorghum or ribbon-cane syrup upon which we floated flecks of butter — that is, if we had butter and if we had syrup. If there was as much as half an hour between breakfast and time for us to leave to catch the school bus, we worked that long in the field. Then we came in, washed up (unless the water bucket was frozen solid), and walked whatever number of miles it happened to be for us to catch the school bus. As hard as our father worked us, to his credit he never kept us out of school during planting and harvesting times as the parents of some of our schoolmates did.

"I didn't get much education and it handicapped me. I don't want the same thing to happen to you," Daddy said. But Daddy wasn't one to complain about his hard lot — he stoically accepted it.

In the afternoon, we would rush home, change clothes, and work in the field until after dark, literally feeling our way home. Even then, there remained chores to be done by lantern's light. After supper, I was too tired to study effectively, and lessons didn't come easily for me. Often, I didn't blow out the lamp until past midnight.

Daddy insisted upon silence at the supper table. "Your biscuits won't digest with all that talking and laughing going on," he would say.

I remember a night when something caused us kids to explode in laughter.

"Go out behind the barn, every one of you, and stay there until you can quit laughing," my father ordered.

It was cold, so we quickly decided we could quit laughing. But no sooner had we returned to the table than our tickle-boxes turned over again. "Get back out there and don't come in 'till I call you," Daddy commanded. When we trooped in an hour later, the table had been cleared. Going to bed hungry was so devastating that even today I sometimes catch myself trying to swallow laughter at the table.

What with the cruel poverty and backbreaking labor, and with the brightest part of my life – going to visit Papa Leslie – dimmed by distance and duties, my young life seemed almost unbearable. And then something (I almost say someone) good came my way. It was a dog, appropriately named "Trouble."

3

trouble lives up
to his name

Earl and I had hoed almost to the pine thicket when we heard the whining. At the edge of the clearing, we saw this bird dog, a brown-and-white pointer. He lowered his head and whined, then raised it and barked as his tail whipped the air.

"He wants to be friends," I said.

Earl threw down his hoe and ran to the dog. I was only five and couldn't keep up with him. Earl dropped on his knees and threw his arms around the dog's neck.

"I've got me a dog! A fine huntin' dog."

"He's mine, too. I saw him same time you did."

"But I claimed him first," Earl said confidently.

"You ain't gonna be able to keep him," I pouted. "Look at that leather collar and chain. He belongs to somebody. They're gonna be out lookin' for him. They'll be mad at you for keepin' him. They might beat you up."

Earl didn't respond. He was too busy trying to avoid the dog's liquid tongue.

"Hey," I said. "Maybe the people that own him won't be mad. Maybe they'll be glad. Maybe they'll pay us a reward."

"Us? They'll pay *me* a reward."

"Earl," I said, growing serious, "you gonna ask Daddy if you can have a dog?"

Earl frowned.

"You know Daddy'll be mad. He'll probably give you a lickin'."

"Then I won't tell him. I'll just chain my dog to this tree and Daddy won't never know."

"Earl, that dog'll have to be fed. You aim to take one of your biscuits ever' mornin' and feed him?"

At last I had Earl where I wanted him. With his bottomless pit, he wasn't about to share food with any dog.

"Guess we'll have to let him go, then."

"Earl," I said, looking him straight in the face, "I'm willin' to feed this dog. Ever' mornin', I'll eat just one biscuit and give my other biscuit to him."

"Gee, would you Mick? That's great!"

"Earl," I said, "I wouldn't do that 'cept the dog'd be *mine*."

He thought for a minute. "Okay, he can be yours. But if there's any reward money, I get half, okay?"

Earl let go of the dog's neck and my own arms replaced his. My own face became the recipient of the slurping affection. My very own dog, and he was so beautiful! He was white with brown on his ears and around each eye. There was a big brown spot on his back, like a saddle, and another brown spot across his hips. Additionally, there were little flecks of brown all over. He had sturdy shoulders, but he was so thin every rib showed.

"I love you," I said, squeezing the dog's neck. "I love you even if you are a mess of trouble. Earl! That's it! I'll call him 'Trouble.' "

"Seems as good a name as any. 'Fore it's all over, I bet you're gonna be in trouble over this here dog."

Earl tied the chain to a sapling. We went to the house and fetched some corn meal mixed with water in a battered pan taken from the chicken yard. Trouble wolfed down the mush. Then I filled the pan with water from a branch nearby.

"You stay here, Trouble," I said. "In the mornin', I'll bring you a nice hot biscuit."

That night at the supper table, I casually asked if we might have a dog someday.

"I can't feed you young'uns, much less no dog," Daddy said. "I had a nice bluetick hound a few years back but had to give him away 'cause I couldn't feed him proper. How come you ask?"

"Oh, no reason a-tall," I said.

Each morning for about a week, I sneaked one of my biscuits into my lap. As soon as we had finished breakfast, I eyed all the plates to see if anyone had left anything. I dashed to the thicket, fed and watered Trouble, and ran home to finish my chores before I could be missed. One morning, I thought Daddy saw me putting the biscuit in my lap, and I felt his eyes following me to the thicket. But if he had caught on, he didn't say anything.

That afternoon, Earl came home from school and joined Daddy and me in the corn patch, where beans were beginning to run up the cornstalks.

"You kids finish choppin' the weeds out of these beans," Daddy instructed us. "I'm goin' up to the house to get my gun and see if I can get us a mess of quail for supper."

I was suspicious and kept my eyes peeled on the thicket. Soon I heard shots, first one barrel and then the other, on the far side of the thicket.

"Earl, you don't suppose. . . ? He couldn't!"

"Yes, he could, Mick. You know how Daddy is."

After a while, I heard the shotgun again, this time in the direction of the pasture. Knowing that Daddy had moved on, I raced to the thicket. Trouble was gone. I glanced about for him, then threw myself on the pine straw and cried.

At dusk, Earl and I went up to the house. Daddy hadn't come yet. Mother got Earl, Mary, and me to the table and held baby Julia to her breast while she herself ate.

In a few minutes, Daddy came in and held up half a dozen quail. "How do you like these birds?" he said proudly. "I'd say they're a good swap for fifteen cents worth of shotgun shells."

"Daddy, while you was huntin', you didn't see a brown and white dog that's been foolin' 'round these parts, did you?" I asked.

"A brown and white dog? Hmmm. Could I have seen a dog like that?"

His mouth and eyes gave him away. My daddy was lying! I burst into tears, jumped up from the table, and ran out the front door.

There, chained to the railing, was my dog.

"Trouble!" I cried. "Oh, Trouble, I was worried 'bout you."

As I hugged the dog, I felt a tap on my shoulder. Daddy stood over me, smiling.

"Mick," he said, "you got yourself a pretty good quail dog."

The next spring, Daddy's boss man, Mr. Rob, moved us to a little shack on his homeplace.

Mr. Rob told Daddy to be sure we knew that the Big House was off-limits to us kids and to our dog. But we hadn't been on Mr. Rob's place more than a month when, one morning, I missed Trouble and suspected he'd gone visiting. I sneaked up to the boss man's barn and ventured inside. "Trouble," I called in a whisper. "Trouble, where are you?"

I found Trouble in a feed trough, his nose yellow with egg yolk. He had found a turkey nest and had eaten perhaps half the eggs.

"Trouble, you bad dog!" I said, smacking him across the nose. Trouble tucked his tail and ran home, yelping all the way. I quickly followed.

That evening, Mr. Rob banged on our door and called Daddy outside. "Was it that damned dog of yours that broke up my turkey nest?" he demanded. "I'll kill that egg-suckin' varmi't!" I went to the door and saw that the boss man had a gun.

"Mr. Rob," I said, "my dog don't eat eggs of no kind,

honest. We made him eat some hen eggs one time and they made him sick."

"That's right, Mr. Rob," Earl said. "Trouble don't eat nothin' but biscuits."

"T'ubble a good dog," chimed in little Mary.

"Well, get this straight," the boss man said. "If I see that dog anywhere around my barn, I'll shoot him." He turned and strode away.

"Mickey," Daddy said, "that's fair enough warnin'. You either keep that dog chained or you won't have a dog."

I kept Trouble tied. In the fields, I fastened his chain to my hoe and he followed me down each row.

But one morning, when I was out by the road with Earl waiting for him to catch the school bus, I heard Trouble yelping and Mr. Rob yelling. I ran to the barn. Trouble was lying on the ground with blood oozing from his nose. Mr. Rob was holding Trouble's chain about midway of its length, and he was flailing Trouble with the loose end.

"No, Mr. Rob! Please don't!" I threw myself atop Trouble and the blow of the chain caught me full force across my shoulders. Expecting another blow, I put my hands over the back of my head.

"Don't kill me, Mr. Rob. Please don't kill me or my dog."

When no blow followed, I dared to look up. I saw a shovel striking Mr. Rob across the side of his head. He reeled across the stall. There was Daddy, standing over him with the shovel raised. Daddy put down the shovel and bent over me. He put his hand against my cheek but quickly withdrew it. His hand was dripping with blood, which he took to be mine. Actually, it was Trouble's.

By now, Mr. Rob had risen to his knees. Daddy kicked him in the chest. For good measure, Earl ran over and socked him on the nose.

"C'mon kids," Daddy said. "Let's get out of here before I kill him."

I was holding Trouble, and Daddy picked us both up and

carried us in his arms. Once home, he deposited me on a bed and Trouble on the back porch. Mother bathed the welt on my back with warm water, then applied baking soda. In turn, I bathed and treated Trouble's wounds.

That afternoon one of Mr. Rob's hired hands told us that it had required nine stitches to close a cut in the side of the boss man's head. The doctor ordered Mr. Rob to stay in bed for a couple of days. Daddy told Mother that Mr. Rob might have him arrested. I feared that just any time the sheriff would come and take Daddy away, but he didn't.

Three days after the incident, the hired hand came and told Daddy Mr. Rob wanted to see him. Mother pleaded with Daddy not to go up to the Big House. She was afraid Mr. Rob might shoot him.

"I can't avoid that man forever," Daddy said.

In a little while, he returned.

"Well, Annie Will, it's just what we expected. We've got to move. We have one week to get off this place, so start packin'."

For Daddy and Mother, this was sad news. The cotton crop was just inches high, and all our work so far would be lost. But for me, the move was good news. I wanted to get as far away from that mean old Mr. Rob as possible. His face haunted me and I kept seeing him whip Trouble with the chain. I even felt the searing blow across my shoulders.

My worst fear was that Daddy would insist we get rid of Trouble. Instead, to my great joy, he declared, "This dog has earned himself a place in our family."

I was overjoyed.

Because our eviction was coming after planting time, there was little prospect that Daddy could find a place for us. Because we were known to be a hardworking, honest bunch, however, people took an interest in our plight. The proprietor of the crossroads store drove over in his wagon to inform Daddy of a possible opening on a farm owned by the president of the bank in Davisville. A sharecropper who faced a felony charge in the spring term of court had moved without giving notice.

We were elated when Daddy returned from talking to the banker and told us we were getting the place. He said there was a good stand of cotton already and some bottom land ready to be planted in corn. But for me the best news was Daddy's casual mention that the new place was only two miles from Papa Leslie's.

On the eve of our move, Daddy came chugging into the yard in an old truck loaned him by the banker. We begged him to give us a spin, but he refused. "It wouldn't be right to use the truck for pleasure," he said.

Mother was big with Bobbie and quite sick, so she couldn't bend or lift. I packed our few canned goods and dishes.

It was raining next morning, but we had no choice but to move. Earl and Daddy loaded the kitchen table, two benches, Daddy's rocking chair, several wooden boxes which served as chairs, a wooden safe with screened doors to keep flies off stored food, the washtub and scrub board, and the heavy iron washpot in which we boiled clothes, made lye soap, and (when we had a hog to kill) cooked out fat. Our dozen chickens were put in a rickety coop. The wood stove stayed; there would be another one at the new place.

Once the truck was loaded, Earl hitched up the mule and set out in the wagon, with the cow and her calf tied on behind. Mother, holding Julia in her arms, and Mary rode in the cab with Daddy. I stayed and helped a neighbor lady get ready for the second load. I was afraid Mr. Rob might come and do us last-minute harm, so I was relieved when Daddy said Trouble could stay behind with us. It seemed an eternity, but in late afternoon I heard the *clackety-clackety-clackety* of the truck. I helped Daddy load our homemade chifforobe, a trunk containing bed covers, and some boxes of odds and ends. Last were our two beds. The mattresses were placed on top of the load to weigh down the boxes. Daddy had brought the chicken coop back. He lashed it on, high behind the cab, and I coaxed Trouble into it. Daddy had a box on the seat with him, so I sat in the back to see that nothing fell off.

Once we were under way, I clambered to the top of the load and stretched out on a mattress. As we jounced along, I felt the mattress slipping toward the rear. Mindful of my responsibility, I clung to the mattress and yelled for Daddy to stop, but the clatter of the engine drowned me out.

Whether we hit an extra large bump or a gust of wind hit us, I don't know. Anyhow, the mattress sailed off the truck with me clinging to it. I seemed to be airborne for an eternity. I recall looking back and seeing Trouble peering out of the coop at me and barking an alarm.

Fortunately, when the mattress landed, I was on top of it. I watched the truck disappear. What if another automobile — maybe mean old Mr. Rob's truck — came along? I tugged the mattress into the ditch alongside the road. It was getting dark and the rain started again. I crawled under the mattress. The ditch was muddy, but the mattress protected me from the cold wind and rain. Soon it was pitch dark and I was frightened.

I learned later that Daddy didn't miss me until he arrived at our new house and jumped out of the cab, calling to me, "Mickey, hop down and help us to get this stuff unloaded and out of the rain." By this time the whole family was around the truck. There was no Mickey. And only one mattress.

"Mickey's fallen off the truck!" Daddy exclaimed. "Let's go back and find her."

Everyone squeezed into the cab except Earl, who sat atop the cargo and scanned the countryside as a sailor might scan the sea for a man overboard.

I heard a truck approaching and thought I heard Trouble barking. When the truck drew nearer, I knew it was my family. I crawled out of the ditch and waved my arms.

"There she is!" Earl cried. Daddy, spotting me at the same time, pushed on the horn. *Ah-ooga! Ah-ooga!*

It was a joyous reunion. Mother was trying to wipe mud

off my face. "What happened, honey?" she asked over and over. Daddy was feeling my arms and legs to make sure I hadn't broken any bones. And Earl was insisting that I describe every sensation I experienced while flying through the air on the "magic mattress."

"Gosh, I wish it could of happened to me," he said.

I broke away and climbed up to greet Trouble, who was barking happily.

"You tried to tell Daddy, didn't you?"

Trouble extended his tongue through the mesh and licked my face and hands.

"This time, Mickey, you'll ride in the cab," Daddy said. And I did.

While Mother cooked supper, I explored the new house. Like all our previous residences, it was only a shack. Holes in the clapboard walls were covered with metal signs advertising soft drinks or chewing tobacco. The roof was rusty corrugated metal. There was no ceiling, no interior finish. There were cracks in the floor that I could stick a finger through. The well water was dingy and odd-tasting.

As always, one of the two rooms served as the kitchen-eating-sitting area, the other as a bedroom. Mother and Daddy slept in one bed, while Earl, Mary, Julia, and I slept in the other. We had to lie crosswise to fit. Although I was young, I recognized that this was a poor excuse for a house. This particular night, however, the pathetic old shack was a welcome refuge.

Mother had prepared an unusually good supper of streak-o'-lean, canned collards, and cornbread. But the best part was, for the first (and last) time, Daddy let us giggle to our hearts' content. We credited this relaxation of the rules to my ride on the Magic Mattress. That lumpy sack of chicken feathers, whose shafts poked through the ticking and prodded would-be sleepers, had done something that all of us kids put together had not been able to accomplish!

Because the Magic Mattress was rain-soaked, we kids slept on the floor. A warm, moist tongue licked my face. It was

Trouble. I lay there stroking my dog and feeling the warm, soft bodies of my sisters on either side of me.

One little lamb had been lost. My father was glad it had been found, and I was terribly glad that he was glad.

I had my family. I had my dog. I was living closer to Papa Leslie's. The drudgery of the fields would remain wherever we went. But I sort of liked this new place.

4

papa leslie
and a man named god

We were hoeing corn in the bottom land and Daddy said
to us, "Hurry and finish the rows you're doin' and we'll stop
and rest a minute. I'll sing 'Old Grizzly Bear' for you."

We loved to get a rest, and we especially loved to have
Daddy sing for us. He would extend his arms and grab us and
pull us up close to him as if he were the old grizzly bear. We
would squeal in mock protest, for this rare chance to be
hugged by our father delighted us.

When Daddy finished his act, I decided to take advantage
of his good humor.

"Daddy, if'n I hoed this whole patch all by myself, would
you let me spend tomorrow and Sunday with Papa Leslie?"

"Why, you couldn't do it. A six-year-old girl-child hoe this
whole patch? That's ridiculous."

"I can! Wanna bet?"

"All right, if you do it, you can go. But nobody's to help
you, understand?"

My family left the patch to work elsewhere. By the time I
had worked to the end of the first row, I wondered if I hadn't
made a foolhardy – if not impossible – bargain. However, I
kept my head down and chopped away. Going to Papa Leslie's
was worth anything, and that's all I let myself think about. I
didn't stop for water or rest.

31

I finished the patch and dragged myself to the house. I was drawing water to wash up when Daddy said, "Mickey, you can't go visit your grandpa. Your mother's sick. You'll have to stay here and help her."

I was crushed. I dumped the tub of water off the porch, then sat on the steps with my head on my knees crying.

"Mickey," my father said, "I know you're disappointed, but that's how life is. Now get up from there and get goin'."

He didn't have to tell me a second time. I got right up. I washed clothes, churned, cooked supper, and straightened things, meanwhile keeping an eye on Julia and tending month-old Bobbie.

Mother got to feeling better and asked Daddy to let me go to Papa Leslie's next morning.

"I'll wake you early," Daddy said. "You do your chores, help with breakfast and the dishes, and I'll take you."

"Hooray!" I shouted. "Hooray! I'm goin' to Papa Leslie's after all!"

Next morning, I flew through my work. I got out of my overalls and put on a flowered dress with matching bloomers. (Both were made out of flour sacks. Mother chose flour and feed sacks with care, and my sisters and I often squabbled over the patterns.) I put my new nightgown in a paper bag. It was a beautiful gown, although it had "Jazz Feeds" printed on the inside of the hem.

"I'm ready, Daddy."

"You better chain Trouble or he'll follow you."

For all of Papa Leslie's virtues, in my eyes he had one fault. He didn't like Trouble. Trouble chased his guinea fowl and bantam chickens.

I fastened my dog and, at long last, Daddy and I were on the wagon headed for Papa Leslie's. It was a clear day and from my perch high above the mule, I could view the wide, green, wonderful world.

As we approached a crossroad, we saw a buggy coming which we recognized to be Papa Leslie's. He came alongside us and I told him I was on my way to spend the night with him. Papa Leslie looked perplexed.

"I'm running an errand," he said, "but climb up here and we'll tend to this business and then go on home."

I got into the shiny black buggy and said goodby to Daddy. Papa Leslie gave Sally a tap with his long whip and away we rolled. People were always trying to trade him out of Sally, a spirited horse with a coat as bright as a new penny. When she cantered, her mane flowed back onto her neck, and she snorted from time to time. In winter, I liked to watch puffs of vapor shoot out her nostrils.

"Papa Leslie, we're on the road that runs past Uncle Moses' house, aren't we?"

"That's right, Baby."

"Can't we stop at Uncle Moses' sometime? I like Uncle Moses. I like the way he laughs and rubs his old hat 'round on his head. And his whiskers are so pretty and white. But how come his eyes are always red and full of tears?"

"That's what happens to you when you get old."

"He seems so lonesome sittin' under his shade tree. Doesn't anybody ever stop and help him pass the time?"

"I reckon they do."

"We're always in such a hurry; you just holler at him and he hollers back at you and we're gone. You're friendly-like with each other, but you never stop."

"Truth is, your daddy doesn't want you to set foot on Moses' place, Baby."

"Daddy says Moses is a 'nigger.' Is Uncle Moses a nigger?"

"Yes, he is. But that don't mean he ain't a decent sort of person. He does things that make people happy."

"How come folks don't call Nar Sis a nigger? She *is* a nigger, isn't she?"

"People have their favorites, that's all."

"I like niggers," I said.

"I do too, 'cept I don't go 'round sayin' so. Some people wouldn't have nothin' to do with you if'n they thought you liked niggers. They'd call you 'nigger-lover.' "

"But I can tell *you* I like niggers, can't I, Papa Leslie?"

"You sure can, child," Papa Leslie said, patting me on my knees. "It'll be our secret."

I got to thinking about Uncle Moses living alone in that little old shack sitting way back from the road. Well, when I got big and grown, I would stop and chat with the old fellow no matter what people said about me. I might even ask him and Nar Sis to marry together.

We were approaching Uncle Moses' place and I hoped he would be out under his tree so I could wave to him. Just before we got there, however, Papa Leslie reined in and directed Sally into the yard of a burned-out homeplace.

"Baby," Papa Leslie said earnestly, "I want you to do somethin' special for me. Will you?"

" 'Course. You know I'd do *anything* for you, Papa Leslie."

"Well, you see, Baby, Uncle Moses is sick. He's got croup or catarrh or somethin' like that. Terrible contagious, you know. I want to go and see if he needs anything. Do you understand?"

"Yes, Papa Leslie. I'm *glad* you're goin' to check on Uncle Moses."

"All right, then. You wait right here till I get back. I'll tie Sally and you can play in the buggy. Or, why don't you gather up acorns and count them in piles of ten? When I get back, I'll check on how good you counted."

Papa Leslie disappeared around the curve and I busied myself counting acorns, but I soon got bored and decided to walk through the woods toward Uncle Moses' house. When I came to the clearing and saw the house, the temptation to go on over there was too strong to resist. As I tiptoed nearer, I heard Papa Leslie and Uncle Moses laughing like everything. I peeked in a window and saw them sitting at a table. In front of them was an earthenware jug like the funny-smelling one in a closet at Papa Leslie's house.

Uncle Moses would take a swig, wipe his whiskers with the back of his hand, and then hand the jug over for Papa Leslie to take a swig. Except for his red, watery eyes, Uncle Moses didn't look sick to me. He did, however, cough each time he took a sip. And Papa Leslie cleared his throat after each swallow. For sure, he was catching whatever it was that Uncle Moses had.

I didn't want to catch anything. Besides, I had promised Papa Leslie I would stay put, so I backed off and ran across the clearing and into the woods. In my hurry, I didn't pay any attention to directions. Soon I was lost. I moved in circles, crossing the same branch many times. It was getting dark. I began running. I snagged my dress on briars, and several times I tripped on roots and fell.

Finally, too tired to move, I sat down and leaned against the trunk of a big tree. Now and then I would call out, "Papa Leslie!" But I heard nothing except the unnerving cry of a screech owl, the demonic call of a chuck-will's-widow, and the breaking of twigs under the feet of some animal. I thought about the old grizzly bear Daddy sang about and wondered if there were beasts like that in these woods. Daddy had said the way to do was to play dead, but I wasn't sure I could.

I heard the padding of feet down by the branch. An animal was sniffing about. I remained ever so quiet. The animal was coming toward me. I stretched out, rigid. I clamped shut my eyes and quit breathing. I was scared silly when I felt the animal's breath tease my hair. Then I heard a whine, and I knew it was Trouble! He had broken his chain and found me. I hugged him and kissed him as we snuggled together.

In a little while, I heard sounds like a person walking in leaves. Trouble's ears perked up and he gave a low growl. I clamped my hand over his mouth. It might be Mr. Rob, and I didn't want to give away our hiding place.

Then I heard a voice: "Oh, dear God, please help a wicked old man find his darlin' baby girl. Please, God, let her be all right. If you'll help me, I'll serve you every day the rest of my life. And I don't care what her daddy says, I'll teach her to be a good Christian."

It was my Papa Leslie's voice.

"Papa Leslie! Here I am!"

"Baby! It's you! Thank God my prayers have been answered."

"We're over here by this tree, Papa Leslie."

"We? Who's we?"

"Trouble and me. Trouble found me. But who is that with you?"

"Ain't nobody with me, Baby," Papa Leslie said, throwing his arms around me. With tears streaming down his face, he held me close to his trembling body. Trouble sat by and whined.

"Oh, I'm so glad you've come, Papa Leslie." There was a long silence. "But who was that 'God' fellow you were talkin' to?"

"We'll talk about God later, but right now you come along with me. Let's get in the buggy and go home," Papa Leslie said, adding: "If'n I can find my way."

Papa Leslie was unsteady, but we heard Sally snorting and found the rig.

Going home, I said, "Papa Leslie, was you and Uncle Moses really drinkin' medicine?"

"Baby! You peeked, didn't you?"

"Yessir," I said sheepishly.

"Well, some people call it medicine. Me'n Uncle Moses call it home brew. But, Baby, don't you never take the first drink of that stuff. It makes people do strange things, yessiree."

"Like what, Papa Leslie?"

"You promise you won't breathe a word to your pa – or Mama Leslie?"

"I won't. Cross my heart and hope to die."

"Well, Baby, I had a few snorts at Uncle Moses'. I didn't want to leave, but after a while, I saw it was gettin' dark. I knew I'd better get home or Mama Leslie would bless me out. I got in the buggy and gave Sally her own head; she knows the way. When I got home and started to get out of the buggy, I found this here sack (the sack with my gown in it) and realized I'd clean forgot about my baby."

Papa Leslie began crying. I put my hand in his. "That's okay," I said. "I know you wouldn't go off and leave me on purpose."

"I went back to that ol' house and you wasn't there. My heart practically stopped on me. I didn't know which way to turn. So I prayed to God. . . ."

"That's what I want to know, Papa Leslie. Who this God fellow is. I ain't never heard about him before. Mr. Rob used to say 'Goddamn' all the time, but that didn't sound like somebody's name. It sounded more like a bad word."

"God's our lovin' Father in heaven," Papa Leslie said, as though that explained it all.

"You don't mean *our* lovin' father, Papa Leslie. You mean *your* lovin' father is in heaven. You know that *my* daddy lives at our house."

"Baby, I'm too tore up to explain things to you right now, but I promised God I would and I will. Your daddy don't have no use for religion, but *you've got to grow up to be a Christian lady*, and I'm gonna see that you do, in spite of your pa. But right now, all I can say is that I asked God where you was and he told me."

"My gosh, God must be the smartest fellow in the whole wide world."

"He is, Baby. He's smarter than any person ever could be."

"Than any *person*? If'n he ain't a person, what is he? Is he some kind of critter, or maybe a ghost?"

"Baby, don't you fret. You can just take Papa Leslie's word for it that God loves you."

When we got home, supper was on the table. Cold. Mama Leslie was powerful mad that Papa Leslie was so late. He didn't tell her the reason, and I wasn't about to.

After supper, Papa Leslie dozed off sitting in his chair.

"He stopped at Moses' place, didn't he?" Mama Leslie demanded of me.

"Oh, you mean that nice old nigger's house, don't you?"

"Land o' Goshen, child, never in my borned days have I seen anybody so loyal to an old reprobate as you are."

"What's a reprobate, Mama Leslie? Is it bad?"

"Some good, some bad. I guess you'd say a reprobate is a stupid old fool. But a *lovable* old fool. Child, let's me and you go to bed and let the old reprobate be."

Mama Leslie smiled, and I put my hand over my mouth and snickered.

I lay in bed with Mama Leslie, feeling cozy and secure. Now and then, I laughed out loud at Papa Leslie's snoring. My mind whirled with questions about God and reprobates. God was a loving father, Papa Leslie said. A reprobate was a lovable old fool, according to Mama Leslie. What was God like? What was a reprobate like? I'd have to ask Papa Leslie in the morning.

5

i give myself to jesus

One afternoon, a car came jouncing into our yard, scattering the chickens and sending Trouble near about into a fit. We kids (except for Julia, who was scared) ran out and gathered around it. Mother joined us, and Daddy came from the barn to see what the ruckus was about.

The stranger was a "minister of the gospel," whatever that was. Mother called him "Reverend," which was stranger still. He said he preached once a month in the little church near us and was looking for someone to clean and dust the inside between meetings and to sweep the yard once a week with a brush broom. He told Daddy he couldn't pay much – only a dollar a month – but he figured we kids could do most of the work under Daddy's supervision.

A dollar a month! Our spirits fell when Daddy said he couldn't spare the time from his farming. But then he said, "Reverend, if you want to hire these kids directly, that'll be all right with me."

We jumped up and down. We were so excited we could hardly remember our instructions. And as soon as his car pulled away, we wanted to dash off and see our new place of work.

"Hey, hold on a minute," Daddy said. "First, we got to have some rules. Nobody's to go over there 'less Earl is with you. And this here job ain't to interfere with your chores in any form or fashion. Another thing, I don't want you comin' home talkin' about that church. I don't want to hear nothin' about it. And I don't want none of you goin' to any of them meetin's, you hear?"

We nodded.

"Now you can go over there a few minutes, but be back before dark."

We ran most of the way. Earl, Mary, Julia, and I were going to get a quarter a month! Earl had said he ought to get more because he was bigger and stronger, but Daddy had said we'd share alike, including little Julia. We knew we wouldn't have a free hand spending all that money, but at least we'd get some things we needed.

Earl and I pulled on the big, thick door and got it open. We went in. I was disappointed. Papa Leslie had told me the church was the home of God and Jesus here on earth. I had expected a warm, friendly place. Instead, it was cold and lonely. The evening sun caused the shadows of the bare tree limbs outside to play on the walls. The place looked down-right spooky. Julia was scared, so I took her hand and led her around as I inspected things.

There were song books in back of each bench. I didn't know there were that many books in the world. The only books I had seen were Earl's school books, the almanac that the man at the drugstore gave Daddy each year, and the books that boss men kept their records in.

There was a big, tall, velvet-covered chair. Obviously, this was where the minister sat, but because God or Jesus might be resting there between services, I said we oughtn't to try it out. Nevertheless, Earl plopped down in it, and when he suffered no ill effects, I tried it. I felt like a queen!

On the stand in front of the chair, I spied the biggest book I had ever seen. I pulled up the piano stool and opened the book. I found a picture of a lady holding a fat little baby. *This is Jesus and his mother!* Until this moment I had lived up to my promise to Papa Leslie not to breathe a word of what he had taught me about God and Jesus, but when I saw that beautiful picture, I knew I had to share the stories which were exploding inside me. I called the others, showed them the picture, and proceeded to relate everything I could remember. I felt sure of myself at first, but their questions stumped me. "I'll have to ask Papa Leslie about that" was my frequent response.

We did our janitorial chores faithfully; we even put jars of wild flowers on the window ledges. Boy, how we'd like to attend one of the services! Earl mentioned that possibility at the supper table, and Daddy said, "You remember our agreement. I don't want to hear anything about services again." Later, Mother told me she and Daddy wouldn't mind us going except that we didn't have any church clothes.

One third Sunday, Daddy wasn't home and Mother was sick in bed. I decided to go to the church and just peek in and see what a service was like. Maybe I would listen outside and learn more about Baby Jesus. Papa Leslie seemed to get God and Jesus all mixed up, and sometimes I couldn't tell which one he was talking about. But the preacher, he would know everything!

I knew my dress was awful, but I didn't mean to be seen. I went to the church early and hid under the front steps. Soon people started arriving. I'd never seen so many dressed-up folks. When everyone had gone in, I got brave. I tiptoed up the steps, sneaked into the vestibule, and commenced to watch the service through the crack in the inner door.

I enjoyed the singing about "washed in the blood of the lamb," although I didn't think I wanted to be washed in sheep blood. Another song that was prettier was about the "rock of ages," which didn't make much sense, either. I kept hoping they would sing "Jesus Loves Me, This I Know," which Papa Leslie had taught me. It was my favorite. My heart jumped up into my throat when the minister opened the Bible and began to read — but I didn't get a thing out of what he read. He talked about a Moses who wasn't Uncle Moses, and then he read about some folks gathered at a place called Pentecost. Later the preacher had two men pass the two big wooden plates. I was glad to see people putting money in the plates because this likely was where our dollar came from.

When the minister began talking again, I grew more interested and sneaked in and sat on the floor behind the rearmost pew. The reverend surely would talk about the Baby Jesus. But he didn't. I was puzzled, then bored. I dozed off, waking with a start when he shouted:

"Jesus is coming again!"

I looked around to see if I could see Jesus.

"Will you be ready?" the preacher demanded. I looked down at my dirty dress. Clearly, I was not ready.

"Only Jesus can take away your sins," the preacher cried, banging his fist on the stand. I believed it because Mama Leslie had said that nobody but Jesus could have made the change that had come in Papa Leslie's life since I got lost in the woods. Nowadays, she said, he didn't go by Uncle Moses' except in a hard gallop.

"Won't you give yourself to Jesus?" I sure wanted to.

"Come right down here and give me your hand signifying that you are giving your life to Christ," the minister exhorted. "It may be your last chance."

Several persons started toward him. I found myself on my feet headed down the aisle. On either side of me, ladies commenced twittering, and menfolk cleared their throats. When I reached the front, the preacher gave me a warm smile and reached out and took my hand. He said to everybody, "We're very happy to have little Miss Mickey Sauls come to us by profession of faith." I didn't know he knew my name! The preacher tried to turn me around to face the congregation, but I was too embarrassed.

The minister read a lot from the back of the song book and from time to time the people joined in. He put his hand down in a bowl and placed it dripping wet on my tangled hair. Water dripped down my collar as he held one hand on my head and raised the other hand toward heaven. "Mickey

Sauls, I baptize you in the name of the Father, and the Son, and the Holy Ghost," he said. Then, after he said something he called the "benediction," he turned to me and said, "Child, I congratulate you on being the first member of your family to become a Methodist!" People started coming toward me. I bolted out the side door and ran home.

I tried to tell myself Daddy would understand, but I knew that he wouldn't. And he didn't. When he got word of my disobeying him, he called me out back and laid the razor strap on harder than I'd ever felt it before.

"You've embarrassed our whole family," he said. "You're not to darken the door of that church again, you understand?"

"Yessir, yessir!"

"You've made a laughin' stock of yourself."

"No sir, nobody laughed at me."

"You gonna do what your daddy tells you?"

"Yessir, yessir!"

I dragged myself off to the cotton shed and flopped down on the cottonseed. My buttocks were on fire. But I also had a warm feeling in my heart — I didn't understand it, but it was there. For the first time following a licking, I wasn't angry with my father. Instead, I felt love for him. And I wanted him to know the love of God and Baby Jesus.

Dear God, thank you for lovin' a pore little girl like me. And don't mind my daddy. He don't mean to be insultin'. He don't know no better. Papa Leslie says if Daddy don't say your name and Jesus' name, he's goin' straight to hell. God, don't send my daddy to hell, please. You'll find he's a nice man when you get to know him. He's just had to work so hard he's always tuckered out. I want you to love my daddy, Jesus — just like you love me and I love you.

My seat hurt, but worse was the hurt of knowing that I couldn't go back to *my* church. Nobody, not even Papa Leslie, had ever smiled at me quite like that preacher did. That preacher — well, I would put him right up there with God and Baby Jesus!

Needless to say, my brother and sisters and I missed that twenty-five cents a month.

On the Saturday following the Sunday when I "made a spectacle" of myself, as Mother expressed it, my prayer for my daddy was partly answered. A Bible salesman came to our house. I expected Daddy to chase him off without giving him a chance to say one word. Instead, he invited the salesman in and listened carefully as each Bible was described. I could see that Daddy was taking a shine to the one with a black leather cover, gold lettering, and the words of Jesus printed in red. There were explanations about things over in the back. And there were nice color pictures – I don't want to forget them. Daddy bent over and studied each one of them.

"Mr. Sauls, in a home blessed with fine children like yours, it'd be a shame not to have a nice Bible like this. It would be an heirloom. Someday, long after you're gone, your children would look at this book and remember you and how you gave them a good start in life."

"Well, I don't know. . ."

"You're thinking about the price, aren't you, Mr. Sauls?"

"Well, as a matter of fact, I was. How much is it?"

"Just forget about the price. It really doesn't matter. What matters is that we have a family easy-payment plan. Each month, I'll drop by and collect the mere sum of one dollar and fifty cents."

A dollar and a half a month! I thought he might as well have said a million.

"Then I'll take it," Daddy said. You could have knocked me over with a feather.

"You'll never regret it," the salesman said. "Now do you happen to have a dollar and a half to put down on this fine Bible?"

Daddy told Mother to get a dollar and a half out of her butter and egg money.

When the salesman had gone, Daddy said to Mother:

"Annie Will, I want you to put this book on the table by our bed, and I don't want the kids touchin' it. It cost too much money to let them tear it up."

How I longed to be able to sit down with that Bible in my lap. I wanted to study the pictures; I wanted to try to figure out some of the words. But I couldn't. Only a few times did I dare sneak a look into that book.

Daddy's hands-off edict added to the mystery of the Bible, and it made me relish the opportunity to take Papa Leslie's Bible in my hands, look at it, feel it, even smell it.

But, somehow, with the Bible in the house, I felt better about Daddy and the threat of him going to hell. Besides, I was sure God and Baby Jesus were glad the Bible was there.

6

and the devil will be the principal

Even today, thinking about grammar school causes a pall of sadness to spread over me. I hadn't been in the first grade but a few days before I decided I was a misfit.

First of all, I didn't like the confinement. I could work as hard as the next kid – in the open – but in a crowded classroom, I couldn't breathe. Confined to my desk, I got fidgety. And I performed poorly. What with housework, cooking, baby-minding, field work, and chores, I never had enough time to prepare my lessons. Occasionally, I dozed off in class and was awakened when the teacher gave me a hard thump on the back of my head.

In those days, nobody had much of anything – but we had nothing! Nobody much dressed up – but I came in patches and tatters (but clean). The teacher said my grammar was atrocious.

"How can I do better when I don't know no different?" I asked her.

At lunchtime, Earl ate his lunch on the back steps smack dab in the middle of the rest of the kids. He didn't care if they saw what he brought in his lunch pail. But I couldn't bear to let my schoolmates see the contents of my pail – usually two biscuits and a little jar of sorghum syrup. I felt crude poking my finger into the biscuit to make a hole to pour the syrup in. Another standard item was a baked sweet potato. Other kids brought potatoes, but usually they had something to go with theirs — ham in a biscuit or fried chicken. I ate my lunch in some bushes at the corner of the school building. At no other time did I feel apartness as acutely as at lunch.

I got along well with the boys, although some of them resented my being able to outrun them or knock a ball farther. And if they gave me a hard time, I slapped the fire out of them. There was no risk of them tattling to the teacher; a boy wouldn't dare complain about a girl getting the best of him.

It was the girls that I couldn't cope with. They were feminine; I was a tomboy. They had manners; I had none. With the boys, I was a born organizer and often was one of the two captains choosing up sides for ball. But the girls gave me a cold shoulder. When boys teased me about seeing my black bloomers, I just grinned, sort of proud they paid me that much attention. But when girls ridiculed my bloomers, I cried.

One day, I came home from school and found a package waiting for me. I was ten years old and in the fourth grade and never in my life had I received a package. This parcel was from Aunt Mary, and when I opened it, there was a *store-bought dress*! It was brown with little pink designs in it. It had a white collar, puffed sleeves, and a gathered skirt. There was a pair of bloomers to match! When I tried it on, it almost made me like being a girl, and even Daddy admitted I looked pretty.

That Friday, because I was going to see Papa Leslie immediately after school, I wore my new frock. It was the first time I had ever felt the least bit feminine. I was so self-conscious, I'm sure I was obnoxious. But secretly I felt proud, and it was the first day of school that seemed to end too quickly.

As we waited for the "second load" bus which would take

me to Papa Leslie's, some of the boys climbed a persimmon tree. The first frost had fallen and the fruit was very sweet. The best ones were always in the top, and on this occasion the boys couldn't reach them. Unable to resist proving my agility, I took off my shoes and swung up, branch by branch, until I was hanging precariously near the very top, shaking the branches as hard as I dared.

One of the girls, Grace Mozeley (I'll always remember her taunting face), started chanting, "Look at the grinnin' possum in the 'simmon tree!" The other girls took up the cry. I was infuriated! I started down to knock their blocks off. But that's all I remember.

I woke up in the doctor's office. I was bruised all over. I had a big bandage on my head — and half of my long, black tresses had been cut off. I had fallen on a sharp stick and it had laid open a jagged wound across my scalp. But what I regretted even more was the fact that the doctor had slit my bloodstained dress to get it off me. I thought I'd never be able to wear it again.

In a few weeks, I was as good as new. But it took much longer for my hair to grow out. And despite Mama Leslie's finest mending, my dress was never the same again.

Later that year, I arrived at school one morning to be confronted in the hall by five girls. Grace Mozeley, the spokesman, came up, hands on hips, and said, "Do you know what we've decided? We've decided that your eyes look like two fried eggs in a slop bucket!"

I hadn't forgiven Grace for the persimmon tree incident, and now this! I grabbed her by the throat and banged her head against the wall. Two of the other girls fought to pull me off her. (The other two had run.) I turned and pushed one girl down, then grabbed the other by the hair. She sank to her knees. "Say you're sorry," I demanded, "or I'll pull every hair out of your head!"

I felt a hand on my shoulder. I was about to swing at its owner when I saw that the interloper was a teacher. I struggled to get my bloomers up from around my knees, and I pinched my nostrils together to stanch the dripping blood.

The teacher marched me down the hall to the principal's office. Taking one look at me, he yanked me into a little room behind his office – a room called "The Dungeon" by boys who had been disciplined there.

"Young lady, I'm going to show you that we don't tolerate this kind of conduct. Bend over that chair!"

I tried to explain how the fracas had started, but he wouldn't listen. He reached up on the wall and grabbed his paddle, which had eight holes bored in it. I didn't count the holes – I knew them by reputation. With the first whack, I shot upright. He shoved me down and held the back of my neck with his left hand while he wielded the paddle with his right hand. I wanted to cry – to scream – but I didn't want him to have the satisfaction of knowing how much he hurt me.

After about twelve licks (most of the boys got six or eight), he let me up. Shaking with rage, I looked him straight in the eye. Then I spit in his face. I ran out of the office and out of the school. Home was nine miles away.

I had gone a mile and a half when I knew I wouldn't make it. My bottom had been numb, but now the pain frightened me. I lay down on my stomach beside the road. Eventually, the school bus would come along. My brother and sisters would be on the lookout for me.

The bus driver stopped. I was one of his favorites because I was able to keep the other kids quiet. When he saw how I was suffering, he muttered, "Why, that dirty, low-down scoundrel!" When we got to our stop, he offered to drive me all the way home, but I told him he needn't bother – I'd be all right. We still had four more miles to walk, and the bus had no more than pulled out of sight when I felt dizzy and passed out. Mary and Julia stayed with me while Earl went to get Daddy.

I had revived when Daddy, Mother, and Earl arrived in the wagon. Daddy had lashed the poor mule most of the way. He told my brother and sisters to sit with their laps lined up to form a couch for me, protecting me from jolts. Daddy lifted me into place, taking care to position me so that nothing pressed against my buttocks. Mother cuddled my head in her lap.

When we got home, Daddy eased me into bed. Mother tried to get my bloomers off, and I cried out in pain.

"Oh, my God! Wade, look at this!"

Daddy took one look and strode out of the house. I heard his "Hii-yahh," then the sound of the mule's hooves and the squeaking of wagon wheels. Mother ran to the kitchen and saw that the shotgun was gone from the wall.

"Oh, dear God, don't let him kill anybody," Mother said.

There were lights on in the schoolhouse, so Daddy went directly there. He burst into the principal's office without knocking. The principal and three other men were seated. One of the men said, "Mr. Sauls, we're having a school board meeting. Is anything wrong?"

"Ask *him* what's wrong!" Daddy shouted, pointing the shotgun at the principal.

The principal blinked.

"Well?" said a board member.

"Today it happened to be my unfortunate duty to have to discipline this gentleman's daughter," the principal said.

Daddy grabbed the principal by the lapel of his coat and shook him. "He beat my daughter unmercifully, that's what he did, gentlemen. Unless you could see my poor little girl, you'd never believe it!"

"Well, we *should* see her, by all means," said a board member. "May we come as soon as we're through?"

They all came to the house. Mother asked if I would let them see where I had been beaten. I had mixed feelings but agreed when Mother said I could put a pillow over my head and pull a sheet up over my legs. When the board members came in, they didn't say anything, but I could sense their reaction. As they turned to leave, one of them patted me on my shoulder and said, "God bless you, child."

I heard the principal trying to apologize, but Daddy would have none of it. "Get out! Get out of this house!" he shouted.

Next day, my brother and sisters came home from school bursting with the news. The principal wasn't there. He had been fired.

I was in bed for two weeks. The sores on my bottom became infected and my legs developed long red streaks which the doctor feared to be blood poisoning. It was touch-and-go for a few days until I improved.

While I was recuperating, two things cheered me. One, Daddy let me read the family Bible whenever I chose. And two, Papa Leslie was my frequent visitor.

Once while Papa Leslie and I were alone, I said, "Papa Leslie, you know how you're always talkin' about people goin' to hell? You say there'll be awful fires and terrible things like that? Well, I've got news for you. Hell is gonna be in the shape of a schoolhouse – and the Devil will be the principal!"

The night I became lost had brought Papa Leslie and me – already close – even closer. Mama Leslie credited me with his "new birth." My presence was good for him, she said. Often, she let on to my parents that she and Papa Leslie needed me for this or that.

Papa Leslie faithfully attended two types of events that I enjoyed immensely. One was fiddlers' conventions, the other his church, which was Primitive Baptist.

Papa Leslie first took me to his church a few weeks after I had joined the Methodist Church. In the meantime, the Methodist minister had stopped by our house. Daddy was polite but cool. What he resented, he explained, was the preacher taking me in without first consulting him and Mother. The preacher, on the other hand, insisted that my baptism was a matter between me, as a child of God, and the Lord.

"Jesus said to let the little children come unto him, and I

aim to do just that," the minister said. "I'm not about to be a millstone around the neck of a precious child. I'm sorry, but that's the way I feel."

"And I don't aim to let a child of mine go near a church that don't have no more respect than that for the rights of her parents," Daddy said. "And *I'm* sorry, but that's just the way *I* feel."

Papa Leslie's church was different. The main thing was, more went on. People prayed out loud and marched around singing. One minute they'd be happy, the next minute crying. The preacher didn't talk like other people. He was always saying "And er-uh . . . and er-uh." He seemed always to be trying to catch his breath but couldn't because he didn't stop shouting. The strangest thing, though, was seeing grown men get down on their knees and wash each other's feet in a basin.

I asked Papa Leslie the meaning of this, and he said it was a "ritual." He told me the story of Jesus washing his disciples' feet. "It's a way to show another person how much you love him."

When I returned home, I told Daddy I wanted to wash his feet. Where had I got such an idea, he demanded. I told him about Papa Leslie's church and the "ritual" in which the men showed their love for each other.

"I ain't got much religion," Daddy said, "but I do know it's wrong for a *man* to love another *man*. I don't want you goin' to your grandfather's house — much less church — any more!"

The next time Papa Leslie came to our house, Daddy asked him straight out: "Ol' man, what do you mean takin' my daughter to that church and fillin' her with that foot-washin' tommyrot?"

Papa Leslie stood right up to Daddy. "Wade," he said, "that girl needs religion. Everybody does, and that includes you. If'n you weren't so derned stubborn, you'd admit your sins and be saved."

Daddy stalked out of the room. I watched him go across

the pasture, kicking cow chips all the way. I thought Papa Leslie had ruined things for sure. But the next weekend, Daddy asked me, "Do you want to go to your grandpa's again this weekend?"

Of course I did!

Papa Leslie had a surprise for me. He had bought a big, thick Bible story book from the salesman who sold us our Bible. Some of the pictures confused or frightened me, and some of the stories about torture and war and God's wrath made me feel uneasy. So, I wouldn't look at the book by myself; instead, I let Papa Leslie read it to me and explain things. He made everything seem just right.

Whereas at home I was awakened by that terrible bell, at Papa Leslie's I was awakened by my grandfather's fiddle. Papa Leslie would sit on the side of my bed and strike up his favorite tune, "Turkey in the Straw." I would open my eyes, stretch, and say, "Papa Leslie, play 'Jesus Loves Me'." He would, and both of us would sing.

I can't remember the first time Papa Leslie took me to a fiddlers' convention. I guess I was five or six. But I distinctly remember a convention that he took me to when I was ten. I was entranced by the Charleston contest, which was a standard event. Until then, I'd never paid any special attention to this competition. On the way home, Papa Leslie said he would teach me to Charleston that night and the next day, and if I would practice hard during the week, he would enter me the next weekend. I said I'd do it. Papa Leslie often won first prize in fiddling, and if I could win first prize in the Charleston, we'd be *some* team!

I practiced hard. When the big night arrived, Mama Leslie got me into a pink crepe-paper costume she'd made and stuck a big, pink crepe-paper flower in my hair. Papa Leslie fiddled "Turkey in the Straw," and I danced just the way he had taught me. We were disappointed when I only got third place, but we didn't give up. Papa Leslie pointed out my mistakes and taught me some new steps. I was more determined than ever.

The next weekend, I won first place. People were clapping, stamping their feet, yelling, and whistling. Until then, few people had ever given me an admiring glance, much less cheered me.

On the way home, I said, "Papa Leslie, winnin' does somethin' for you, doesn't it? I mean, tonight I felt like *somebody!*"

"Child, you don't know nothin'. You can't imagine what the cheerin' does when you're a wore-out ol' man like your grandpa."

"Papa Leslie, I've just made up my mind. I'm gonna become the Charleston champion of the whole dadburned United States of America!"

I expected him to pooh-pooh the idea. Instead, he said, "And you can do it, too, if you just put your mind to it!"

On several occasions, I took first place again, and Papa Leslie announced that I was ready for the Greer County Fiddlers' Convention. And I *was* ready. I came away with the grand title of "Queen of the Charleston." The announcer made a big to-do over the fact that I was only ten years old.

In the buggy going home, I said, "Well, what's next, Papa Leslie?"

"Well, your majesty, I humbly suggest that we try some new things."

"Like what, for instance?"

"Oh, like singin', givin' readings, things like that."

For the next couple of weekends, we practiced two songs that Papa Leslie had taught me long before. One was called "I Want To Wake Up in the Morning" and the other was "Pretty Mickey." We went to a box supper, and after the frilly boxes of delicious food had been consumed, someone asked Papa Leslie to play his fiddle and me to do the Charleston.

"If it pleases you," Papa Leslie said, bowing, "I would prefer to introduce the 'Thrush of Persimmon Grove.' " The crowd applauded. My grandfather put me up on a table and I sang my song. I brought the house down. There were cries of

"More!" I looked expectantly at Papa Leslie, but he shook his head. I whispered in his ear, "I could sing 'Jesus Loves Me.' " Again, he shook his head.

When we got outside, I asked him why he had acted like that, and he said, "Baby, an important rule of the entertainment world is to leave your audience beggin' for more." I promised to remember.

Papa Leslie also taught me a poem about a poor rag doll, which I recited while acting the part of the doll. People dabbed their handkerchiefs to their eyes. I soon recognized that an entertainer possesses power — power to make people either laugh or cry. I was ten years old, born in a cotton patch to dirt-poor parents, and living in a house without a stick of store-bought furniture. I was a *nobody* — yet being able to sing, dance, and give recitations turned me into a *somebody*. I liked that sort of magic.

For every excursion into the clouds that I made with Papa Leslie, however, there was a return trip home which brought me crashing back down to reality.

One afternoon, a well-dressed matron from Davisville, a Mrs. Elmo, came to our school to arrange lessons in music appreciation. When she asked who would be interested, I was the first to get my hand up. Mrs. Elmo noted my name, along with half a dozen others.

"Our lessons will be weekly, at a time to be arranged. You will learn to read notes, to sing, and to appreciate good music. You will also become familiar with the various instruments."

I wanted to tell her I already sang in public and was familiar with the fiddle — or violin, as she called it. She dismissed us before I had a chance to speak.

I was elated over this new opportunity to expand my entertainment career. I could see myself becoming a choir soloist, opera singer, or organist in a motion picture theater. While the projectionist changed reels, I could play the organ, sing, do the Charleston — even throw in a reading if there remained time to be filled.

On Monday, our classroom teacher announced that the

music lady would be there Friday afternoon at 1:30. When that magic time arrived, we went to an empty room. Mrs. Elmo came bouncing in and started us with breathing exercises: "Come up on your toes, breathing in all the way. Now, ease back down, breathing out. Very good!"

This seemed silly, and I was glad when she opened a box and took out a stack of red books. She distributed these and said: "Be sure to write your name on the inside cover so that your book doesn't get lost." Painstakingly, I printed my name. I was admiring my name in that handsome book when she said: "Now pay strict attention! Next Friday, each of you bring a dollar to pay for your book."

A dollar! Why, she might as well have told me to bring her the moon. I turned around in my desk and asked Pearl Spinks if I had heard correctly.

"Yep, that's what she said, all right."

I looked down at the book. Those two words, "Mickey Sauls," looked enormous. Then Mrs. Elmo added: "You should also inform your parents that the lessons will be fifty cents each."

That did it!

At the supper table that night, in a well-chosen moment, I announced that I was enrolled in music appreciation.

"Mickey, that's real good!" Mother said.

"And it's only going to cost fifty cents a week — plus a dollar for the book, of course."

Daddy's fork dropped into his plate and clattered about for what seemed a terribly long time. "It's *only* going to cost *what*?" he exclaimed. "Haven't I told you never to let me hear you say *only* a nickle or dime — and you sit there and say *only a dollar!*"

I slipped out of my chair and was leaving the table when he whipped his belt out of its loops and gave me a good whack across the seat. "If you think that money grows on trees, I'll teach you different."

I didn't get to finish my supper — a supper that, incidentally, I myself had cooked.

The next Friday, after all the other pupils had left the room, I reluctantly surrendered my music book to Mrs. Elmo, explaining that my daddy said there was no way I could get a dollar, much less the fifty cents every week for lessons.

"Very well," Mrs. Elmo snippily replied. She rummaged around in the regular teacher's desk, found a bottle of ink eradicator, and spread the solution over my name. While I sadly watched over Mrs. Elmo's shoulder, my name vanished. And so did my dreams for a music education.

7

the great depression

In 1932, I was fourteen years old, in the ninth grade, and commuting between two worlds. One of my worlds was the world of fantasy. During the Great Depression, this world was crowded, for few persons (my father was an exception) found themselves built of strong enough stuff to accept the harshness of the realities about them. My other world was the "Sauls Family Chain Gang," as we kids surreptitiously termed ourselves. I hated this latter world, not only because it blistered my hands (and, at times, my seat), broke my back, and baked my brain, but also because it taunted my dream world and called it a lie.

At age fourteen, I was physically more mature than most of my classmates. This was a mixed blessing. I didn't like being different from the other girls, because they often made fun of me. I didn't understand the changes that came with adolescence. This was for me a time of anxiety and fright. I was totally ignorant when it came to my anatomy and physiology, and I had nobody to confide in or explain things to me. On the other hand, there were advantages to having a well-developed body. The boys noticed me in a different way now, and I craved all the attention I could get.

My aspirations to become a movie star also caused me to relish my metamorphosis from a flabby child into a fledgling adult, complete with a beautiful body. I had long since abandoned picturing myself as a transparent "Little Miss Sunshine." I wanted to become an alluring, complicated, very adult dramatic star. My cocksureness about what I wanted out of life widened the gap between me and my contemporaries, most of whom had only vague or imposed notions of what they wanted when they grew up.

In the summer of 1932, I discovered movie magazines. I couldn't afford them, although Papa Leslie occasionally gave me money to buy one. Instead, when school started, I traded pears from our farm for magazines that other girls had already read.

My idol was Joan Crawford. I read and clung to every available word about her. We had much in common, I felt. First, she got her break into the movies because of her dancing talent. She danced the *Charleston*. She had won a hundred cups in competition, and since I myself had gathered quite a few, I saw myself fast becoming a Joan Crawford.

We had the same strong will. Joan Crawford knew she was *somebody*, yet she strived for higher levels of greatness. I hung upon the wall of my inner being her words: "I must never allow myself to become self-satisfied. But I don't think I ever will. My ambition is too driving — too relentless — to permit me to grow complacent."

Also, I admired her for supporting her mother and kid brother. I myself had visions of snatching my own parents and brother and sisters out of their shack in the Land of Nothing to establish them in a mansion in the Land of Plenty.

And, last, Joan Crawford had a sex image that I felt comfortable with. When I tried to conjure up visions of myself as a Jean Harlow or Ann Sheridan, my projections left me anxious. Joan wasn't sickeningly sweet or excessively feminine. Yet, in real life she won Douglas Fairbanks, Jr., and Franchot Tone, and in films there were always the Gary Coopers and Clark Gables fighting over her. I liked the way she viewed their antics with cool detachment.

Back in 1929, Aunt Mary had taken me to Macon to see

the silent film *Our Dancing Daughters*. After that, on occasions when work in the fields became unbearable, I would recreate in my mind the scene where Joan does the Charleston. She whips off her skirt and finishes the dance in her slip.

"You want to take all of life, don't you?" her boyfriend says.

"Yes – all. I want to hold out my hands and catch at it."

My world of fantasy was a beautiful world, and I wanted to hold out my hands and catch at it. But the truth was, as I grew prettier and more accomplished, I also grew poorer, and the demands made upon me by my family increased. The net effect was to realize that the odds for success were stacked against me. I would never make it to the top if I let my determination flag or if I vascillated about the cost. I didn't intend to waver. I would pay the price, no matter how high it might be.

In regular succession, there arrived another mouth to feed, and, potentially, another pair of hands to grasp a hoe. In 1932, our roster was: Earl, 16; Mickey, 14; Mary, 12; Julia, 10; Bobbie, 8, and Angel 3. (Several years earlier, Roy Russell died of polio at age five. My parents had tried unsuccessfully to get him into a hospital. His illness and lack of proper care caused me to question the goodness of both God and my fellow men. His death broke our hearts. But God soon sent another child to fill the void, and Mother named her Angel.)

As our family increased, my father periodically moved us to larger acreages and larger burdens. We girls tried to do a boy's job. We were motivated not only by our own recognition of our dire need and by my father's razor strap, but also by snide remarks such as: "Well, Wade, if the stork hadn't of played tricks on you by bringin' all them girls, you'd be a man of means, wouldn't you?"

Daddy continued being a tenant farmer, for in spite of our labor and our skimping, we couldn't manage to save anything. In 1930, the drought ruined us. In 1931, we planted every available inch of land in cotton – and by harvest time the price had fallen to five cents a pound! We didn't make enough to pay our bills. After the harvest, Daddy moved us to a still larger farm near a settlement named Henry Springs. That vast expanse of cultivated land alarmed me. But more distressing was our being twenty miles from my dear Papa Leslie's house. We were so hard up that Daddy made us pick back over the cotton fields, which had already been harvested once by our predecessors. The sharp, dry bolls tore into my hands. I couldn't manage more than twenty pounds a day.

So disreputable was the old house that I never brought a friend home from school. Still, the word got out that I was living in a "nigger shack" — a fact which Grace Mozeley publicized in history class one day. (Mother said that a decent black family wouldn't live in it.) There were no screens. Two shutters were nailed shut; the other shutters fit poorly, and some hung by only one hinge. There were gaps in the floor.

The worst part was the mice and rats. I wasn't afraid of mice, so it fell my lot to chase them out of any place they were discovered. But I was terrified by the rats, especially after old Trouble cornered one and lost a plug out of his nose. I lay awake listening to rats running along the open rafters, down the walls, and across the floor. Any minute, one might crawl under the covers with me — or attack my own nose. The rats in the barn were so ravaging that on rainy days when there was no work in the fields, Daddy invited neighbors to come over for a "rat killin'."

The rats and mice created another problem — snakes. On a farm, you learn early that where you find rats and mice, you also find snakes. Snakes were everywhere. Since snakes are good ratters, Daddy wouldn't let us kill anything but moccasins and rattlers.

One chilly night, we were at the supper table. The kerosene lamp was burning brightly, and the wind blowing through the cracks in the floor and walls caused the flame to leap about. I was absently watching the dancing flame when a dark form crashed onto the table. A five- or six-foot black snake had fallen off a rafter over us. Dishes, biscuits, and people scattered in every direction. The snake's body hit the hot lamp globe, causing a singeing sound and odor. As the snake writhed in pain, it knocked over the lamp, breaking the glass and causing flaming kerosene to spill over the table and onto the floor. The eating area soon became an inferno. Daddy ran to get bed clothes to try and smother the fire, but we all had to retreat.

"Oh, the Bible!" I screamed. I ran back into the house and tried to make my way into the bedroom. My father grabbed me and pulled me out of the house. Seconds later, the roof caved in.

We huddled, watching the rich timbers of the old house burn. I didn't mind seeing the house itself consumed — that was good riddance. But except for the clothes on our backs and our few animals, we had lost everything we possessed in this world. It seemed unfair for one family to have as much trouble as we had experienced — sickness, injuries, crop failures, and now this fire.

God, how can you do this to us? I even wonder if you're real. Papa Leslie says you are, but he's an old man tryin' to get ready to die — and me and my family are tryin' to get ready to live. Oh, God, we want to enjoy some nice things like other people do. Papa Leslie says you're a lovin' God. Well, it isn't very lovin' to let our house burn down. We may not be a churchgoin' family, and I know Papa Leslie says you're gonna knock Daddy down if he keeps on denyin' Jesus Christ as the way to salvation, but God, surely you wouldn't get back at him like this! Oh, God, I don't know what to believe. I'm so confused and frightened.

The conflagration brought people from miles around. Some were merely curious, but most came to help. Strangers and acquaintances alike brought food and clothing. Mr. John, Daddy's new boss man, told him that he had a hundred dollars worth of insurance on the old house and Daddy was welcome to the money. And he said if that wouldn't buy enough household goods and other things to get us started again, for Daddy to go into town and buy things on credit and tell the merchants Mr. John would back us. He would let us have another old house on the same place to live in until he could make better arrangements for us.

The next day, Papa Leslie came. Mother sent Mary to the field to fetch me. I ran to Papa Leslie and buried my head in his chest. For several minutes, neither of us said anything — we didn't have to. Then I led him out into the backyard.

"I've got to talk to you," I said.

He leaned against the barnyard fence. "What's eatin' on you, Baby?"

"Papa Leslie," I said, "you've got to explain to me how God can let somethin' like this happen. If you can't, I'm through with God — I'll have nothin' else to do with him."

"But, Baby, this wasn't somethin' that *God* did to you."

"I think it was. You yourself told me that God has a hand in everything that goes on in the world. And it was a *snake* that caused our fire, remember? I think God caused that snake to drop off that rafter just like he made a snake appear to Adam and Eve. God did it to punish us — or maybe just to punish Daddy."

"Baby, the trouble is you are just lookin' at the fire all by itself. What you have to remember is, all — get that, *all* — things work for the best to them that loves the Lord. You love the Lord, don't you?"

"I want to. I've tried powerful hard, you know that."

"All right, look at the full picture. Think about how good your new boss man has been to you and how people that you hadn't seen before have come and helped you. If it hadn't of been for that fire, you would have growed up without knowin' how many friends you have in this world. You'd a growed up not knowin' that although people have a lot of natural devilment in them, they've also got a lot of good in them. This fire may work out to be a blessin'. I know it's hard to accept, Baby, but you have to keep trustin' in the Lord."

Papa Leslie made things sound right. I felt good inside. But the good feelings didn't last. I began finding flaws in his explanation. I found it harder to pray to God. Seeing Papa Leslie so infrequently, I no longer had someone to help me find answers to my questions about God and living a life of faith. I had lost the main source of my spiritual strength. Daddy was too busy to take me to visit Papa Leslie, and Papa Leslie's health was failing fast. He suffered a congestion of the lungs and pains in the stomach known as "adult colic." He didn't feel up to the long drive to our place, and often Mama Leslie wouldn't let him attempt it. "We'll find you dead in that buggy," she said.

So, the year 1932 found me not only in physical poverty, but in spiritual poverty as well. Did God really care? If he did, our house wouldn't have burned. We wouldn't have to scratch for a living. And he wouldn't let a good, God-fearing, generous old man like Papa Leslie suffer.

The next year brought little change except that I was one year older and was expected to do even heavier work. In the late summer, after we had picked our own cotton, Daddy hired Earl and me out to the boss man to pick afternoons and Saturdays.

One evening, we continued picking by the light of the moon. We didn't stop until 9 p.m. Dog-tired, I watched the straw boss and a hired hand lift a huge sheet containing my day's cotton and hook it on scales hung from the rear of the boss man's wagon. The straw boss tapped the indicator outward along the beam and announced, "One hundred and forty-three pounds. Mickey, you done good. We'll just make it an even one-fifty, okay?"

"Sure, Mr. Henderson. Thanks."

What difference does it make? It doesn't matter. Nobody cares how hard I work or how tired I get. It just doesn't matter. Someday I'll leave all this. Someday I'll be somebody!

If you had seen this bedraggled girl, huddled on her empty cotton sack in a desolate south Georgia cotton patch on a stagnant night, you might have asked, "*She's* going to be *somebody*? How pathetic a prayer, how ludicrous a hope."

It didn't make sense, and I knew it.

Somebody? Fat chance. How do you get off a tenant farm? How do you escape imprisonment in peanut and cotton fields? How do you free yourself from laborin' from before daylight 'til after dark? God, I hate this life. I hate it!

I often felt this no-way-out desperation. There was no future for even a bright, pretty girl if she happened to be born to a sharecropper. I didn't want to follow in my mother's footsteps. Her life was a relentless progression of new babies and old tenant houses. How could she possibly turn one of these unpainted shacks into a "home"? How could she, day after day, find the courage to cook those meager rations and then call the resulting grub "dinner"?

No, dear God, that kinda life's not for me. I'm gonna be somebody!

I brushed my long, black hair out of my eyes and wiped the tears away with the hem of my dress. A wind came up and stirred the pine trees, picking up their turpentiny scent. The air dried the damp smudges on my cheeks.

At thirty-five cents a hundred, I had earned fifty-two cents. In a way I felt uneasy making that much money. The black hired hand helping with the weighing — a man with a wife and five children to feed — ordinarily earned a wage of only fifty cents a day. My back, however, told me I had earned that fifty-two cents.

Earl turned in 215 pounds for the day.

"You want me to knock off the fifteen or pay you, Earl?"

"Pay me if it's all right, Mr. Henderson. A penny's a penny. It'll buy me a Baby Ruth."

It being Saturday night, our week's earnings were totaled. Mine came to $1.50. I folded the dollar bill tightly around the half dollar and tied the wad in a corner of my bandana. Daddy would get $1.25 of that money, but the quarter that I would be allowed to spend seemed almost worth my labor.

I had a friend named Ida Harmon, who lived about two miles from us. Her father went into Davisville every Saturday to sell a little produce and buy a few groceries – but mostly to hang around talking politics. Daddy considered such loitering immoral; nevertheless, on those occasions when our work load wasn't too heavy, he permitted me to ride into town with Ida in the rumble seat of Mr. Harmon's roadster. That's where the quarter came in. Ida and I spent Saturday afternoons seeing a shoot-'em-up and the serial – twice. I would have preferred more sophisticated movies, but they played during the week, so I never saw them. Instead, I read about them in the movie magazines.

Still, the westerns weren't all that bad. I liked the way the heroines got by without having to engage in heavy romancing with the cowboy hero. Usually the film ended with the pair holding hands and looking at each other like two sick calves, while the hero's sidekick stood by and grinned. That, or else the hero said goodby and rode off into the sunset. Sometimes I thought I wanted to be a sultry leading lady, but basically I wasn't sure I'd feel comfortable getting into a clinch and receiving one of those head-wrenching kisses that lasted an eternity.

I loved the serials, which continued for eight or ten weeks, each installment ending with the stage coach about to crash over the cliff or an Indian about to relieve the hero of his scalp. Ida kept me posted on the episodes I missed.

That payday night, as I rode home behind Earl on the mule, my mind drifted off to the movies and how good it would be when the picking season was over and I'd get to go see a show again. "Hey, Mick," Earl called out. "It's Uncle Jim's car!"

I slid off the mule and raced into the house. I loved Uncle Jim, who had many of Papa Leslie's qualities. He was handsome, mannerly, gentle, and affectionate. I hoped Aunt Mary was with him. Her confidence in me never failed to brighten my spirits. Papa Leslie told me that I could amount to something, but he spoke in general terms; Aunt Mary, on the other hand, was practical and always full of specific ideas and strategies.

"Well, if it isn't my Pretty Mickey," Aunt Mary said. "I've got some exciting news for you. The Talent Scouts are going to be in Macon next weekend, and I want you to compete."

"Talent Scouts?"

"Yeah, like the Major Bowes' Amateur Hour. The Talent Scouts people will audition performers Saturday morning, and the best will compete in a talent show at the Rialto Theater Saturday night."

My heart pounded with excitement. "Do you think I'd have a chance? What would I do? What would I wear?"

"You would sing *your* song, 'Pretty Mickey,' of course. And I bought you an outfit in Atlanta. I believe it will fit, although we may have to let the blouse out a little in the shoulders."

"It sounds like a mighty good chance," Mother said. "What do you think, Wade?"

Now that I was fifteen, in the tenth grade, and wanting to go places and do things, I often found my mother coming to my aid in support of schemes that Daddy didn't even want to discuss — like the Saturday afternoon movies. Mother, a tiny woman who was dwarfed by my lanky father, was the typical unliberated wife, and her new boldness surprised me. Still, she was careful not to push Daddy too hard, and she never gave him an ultimatum. I was even more surprised when, on occasion, my father relented. This time, I held my breath to see what his reaction would be. I felt that with the cotton-picking season not yet ended, he would certainly refuse.

"Well," Daddy said, "I reckon that with Mary and Jim to look after her, it'd be okay."

I could hardly believe my ears!

Uncle Jim, who was a traveling salesman, and Aunt Mary (who still worked in Atlanta) were vacationing together at Papa Leslie's. Every afternoon that week, Uncle Jim took me from school to Papa Leslie's, where Aunt Mary accompanied me on her piano, drilled me in my song, and showed me how to walk on stage, bow, and all that.

Early Saturday morning, the three of us set out on the 120-mile trip to Macon. My full, orange skirt and frilly, white blouse were packed and my orange parasol stowed, but Aunt Mary indulged my wish to wear the broad-brimmed straw hat which she had dyed orange to match my skirt. Typical of "drummers," Uncle Jim was full of jokes, and the car rocked with laughter and good spirits. Between jokes, Aunt Mary talked about the step that would follow my winning first place that night. Each time, the speculation grew grander.

"Mickey, your daddy is going to be *so* proud of you!" she said over and over. (I hoped so!) Then she'd say, "Maybe you'd better run through the song one more time to make sure you've got it."

By the time we neared Macon, my throat had become scratchy, and Aunt Mary had become as nervous as a cat. It was already twelve-thirty and the auditions would close in half an hour.

"Give it a heavy foot," she said to Uncle Jim. And to me, "Sing that song one last time."

I opened my mouth to sing. Only a croak came out.

"Mickey! Now don't you start that!" Aunt Mary demanded. She made Uncle Jim stop the car. She went into her suitcase and brought out a bottle of mouthwash. Handing it to me, she ordered, "Take a big swig and gargle deep. And Jim, if you don't get us to the theater in ten minutes, your name is mud."

The car roared down the highway. I gargled, then leaned over the side to spit.

"My hat! My hat!" I yelled. The hat was fluttering down the road.

"For God's sake, Mickey, you don't have as much sense as a last year's jaybird," Aunt Mary bellowed. "Turn this thing around, Jim."

Uncle Jim retrieved the hat. Aunt Mary inspected it and muttered something I couldn't make out. Then, grasping the brim in both hands, she tore the hat in two and tossed the pieces out the window.

"Oh, my hat! My pretty hat!" I cried.

Not another word was spoken until we parked in front of the theater. It was 12:55. There wasn't even time for me to put on my costume.

When we rushed into the empty theater, a man down front inquired, "Are you Mickey Sauls?"

I nodded and gave him one of my plastic smiles.

"Well," he said in an exasperated voice, "let's hear it."

Aunt Mary plopped down at the piano, played the introduction of my piece, and then nodded to me. My throat felt like somebody had poured creosote down it. "Mi-mi-mickey . . . Pret-pret-ty . . . M-m-mic-key . . . ."

From that point, I sobbed to the music instead of singing to it.

"Good God!" the man said, looking at Aunt Mary with disgust. Whatever prompted you to bring *her* for an audition?"

"Now you just hold your horses one dad-burned minute," Aunt Mary exploded. "We just got here! You don't expect this child to come running in here at the last minute and do perfect, do you?"

"Sir," Uncle Jim added, "I'd suggest you keep a civil tongue in your head."

The man (who never did introduce himself) relented. "Okay, let's try it again from the top."

I had read that term in the movie magazines and I was impressed hearing it in a real-life situation.

I wanted so much to please, but I croaked!

"That's it! That's it!" the man said. "I can't use her. Get her out of here!"

I burst into tears. Aunt Mary bumped me along as we stumbled up the aisle and out of the theater. Uncle Jim was silent.

On the way home, Aunt Mary grumped about spending all that time and money on me. "Opportunity knocked, but you blew it!" she said.

"But I didn't mean to."

"I know you didn't, honey, but you blew it just the same and it's hard to take."

Uncle Jim suggested, "Why don't you lie down on the back seat and get yourself a nap, Mickey? You'll feel better."

When I awoke, we were in heavy fog. As I sat up, Uncle Jim turned and looked back at me. "Did you get a good nap?"

At that instant the road curved, and we were in the blinding glare of another car's headlights. Aunt Mary screamed. There was the grinding of metal on metal . . . the shattering of glass . . . silence.

Mother was sitting beside the bed. We were in Papa Leslie's room. I was too sore to move. And I had a terrible headache.

"Am I gonna die?" I asked.

"Now, darlin', you're gonna be fine. You banged the back of the front seat with your head. It'll take a few days for you to get up and about, but don't worry about that now."

"And Aunt Mary?"

"She's just fine," Mother said.

Her lips quivered. I knew something terrible had happened.

"It's Uncle Jim, isn't it? Uncle Jim's bad hurt."

Mother put her hands on my shoulders. "I don't quite know how to tell you this, honey, but Uncle Jim is dead."

"Uncle Jim? Dead?"

"Yes, dear."

"Oh, no! Then it was *me* that killed him!"

"Mickey! That isn't true. You know it isn't."

"It *is* true, though! If it hadn't been for me, we wouldn't have gone on that trip. And it was me he was talkin' to when it happened."

I began to sob uncontrollably. Mother brought Papa Leslie in to comfort me. He did the best he could. Uncle Jim had done more living than most people do in twice the time, he said. He had lived a good life and was assured a place in heaven, and eventually all of us would meet him there, he said, adding, "and, Baby, it won't be long before your Papa Leslie will be there with your Uncle Jim." Tears welled up in his eyes.

"Papa Leslie! Don't talk like that!" I protested. But for the first time ever, I saw that my grandfather was, indeed, a very old man — and a very *sick* old man.

"We have to be brave, Baby," Papa Leslie said. "God feels for us. He knows how I feel because he himself lost a son once. I shouldn't be upset. It was God's will for Uncle Jim to go and live with him now. I shouldn't question God's will."

"Papa Leslie, I don't mean to argue, with you feelin' so sad, I mean. But remember? You said God didn't burn down our house. Now how come you say he took Uncle Jim away? That's worse than burnin' down somebody's house!"

I heard little of what Papa Leslie said. I couldn't identify with his stoic resignation. My feelings were more like Mama Leslie's. Over and over, she said, "I just can't understand why a fine young man like Jim had to come to such a terrible end. He had so much to *give* to the world!"

I was perplexed. Was God sitting up there in heaven, looking on disinterestedly while his toy-like creatures suffered mishaps like banging into each other in automobiles? Or were these incidents part of his plan? I couldn't reconcile the concept of an all-powerful God with the misery that I saw people suffering.

If Papa Leslie could find comfort in his faith, well and good — he needed all the comfort he could find. But as for me and my anguish, I certainly didn't feel that God was very near.

8

college and
the impossible dream

During the next two years, I entered every contest that I could. I won the Miss Greer County competition handily, but when I arrived in Warm Springs for the Miss Georgia Pageant and met the other contestants, I knew I was in over my head. These were girls from cities – Atlanta, Augusta, Columbus, Macon, Savannah. Girls with grace, poise, and confidence, and years and years of ballet, modern dance, and drama. Girls who had been coached, preened, and costumed.

I recognized myself to be an awkward country girl, with no training except what Papa Leslie and Aunt Mary had given me. I was seventeen and a high school senior, while most of the other girls were college coeds and a year or two older.

My gown was the prettiest I'd ever had, but because Mother and Aunt Mary had selected the pattern and Mama Leslie had made it, I feared it wouldn't compare with the other girls' dresses, which had been selected in consultation with fashion directors of Atlanta department stores. My bathing suit was almost identical to the other girls' suits – a plain, white "tank" suit. By modern standards, it was modest, but because Daddy had said, "It leaves you practically naked," I felt completely undressed in it, and I'm sure my uneasiness showed.

My strong point was my song, "Pretty Mickey." I had sung it and danced the Charleston to it a thousand times. Also, I had found that people were captivated by the name in the song being my own name, lending a personalized flavor to my act. I wore a short dress with a wide collar and wide cuffs, and my parasol and black patents completed the "little girl" effect.

A few hours before the pageant, my already shaky confidence suffered another blow. While Aunt Mary was away on an errand, I decided to take a dip in the hotel swimming pool. When Aunt Mary returned, she was furious.

"How could you?" she demanded. "Now you won't be able to do a thing with that hair!"

Once I got it dried and combed, I liked it. "It gives me a – well – a carefree look," I said, giving it a whirl.

"A carefree look isn't what we need to go with *that* outfit," she complained.

For the first time in my life, I went into a contest feeling I wouldn't win first place. I wasn't going to be Miss Georgia, much less Miss America.

As the contest progressed, I found myself sitting as one of five finalists. Naturally, my hopes returned. The second runner-up was named, then the first runner-up. That left three of us. Was it possible that I could be the big winner? A minute later, the new Miss Georgia was announced, and I realized that I wasn't a winner at all.

I stood aside, clutching a bouquet of roses, which had been handed me by the emcee, and which I watered with my tears. All the glory belonged to Miss Georgia and the two runners-up. I was glad that only Aunt Mary had come with me. I'd been spared the embarrassment of having my family watch me fail. However, I still dreaded having to tell Papa Leslie.

I perked up when the pageant photographer and the press photographers had me pose with Miss Georgia and the other finalists. And I was delighted when a photographer from one of the Macon papers wanted a shot of me alone. The publicity eased the hurt of not getting a trophy.

Aunt Mary was a scrapper. Backstage, she critiqued my performance. Meanwhile, my mind drifted to my own evaluation of what had gone wrong.

It had been all right to be "country" while singing "Pretty Mickey," but it wasn't all right to be country in an evening dress or swim suit. I resolved to go home and work on poise, polish, and confidence. An overheard remark had given me a cue which was to help me tremendously in future contests. One of the male judges said to another about the winner: "Wow, when she looks at you, she looks you right in the eyes. She makes you feel that you and she are the only two persons left on earth — and you're a *man* and she's a *woman*!" In the future, I might appear demure, but I would never again project insecurity. I would look 'em straight in the eye!

As Aunt Mary and I were leaving the auditorium, the pageant photographer, a quiet, nice-looking fellow with a pleasant way of getting the poses he wanted, called to me.

"Miss Sauls, could I speak with you a moment, please?"

He introduced himself. He was Ken Stambaugh, and he was going to make a movie in the mountain country around Cornelia, Georgia. It would be the first talking picture ever made in the state. Would I be interested in a part?

Would I!

"You're the leading lady I've been searching for," he said. "You look the part and you have just the right shade of accent."

He gave me his card and promised I'd hear from him within a week or two. His parting words were: "And don't you cut that beautiful, long hair."

When I got home, I hurried to tell Papa Leslie the great news. Better than becoming Miss Georgia . . . better than becoming Miss America . . . I was going to star in a movie!

"Mickey," he said, "God wants you to be *somebody*. It's his plan. I've felt it in my bones ever since you were a little bitty girl."

Thank you, God, for everything. I promise to try to live

*up to the opportunities you're sendin' my way. Please forgive
me for ever doubtin'.*

Daddy planned to drive me over to Papa Leslie's the next
evening, but that afternoon the doctor came to our house.

"Mickey, your granddaddy is mighty low. He's been calling
for you. Since I'm a doctor, I want him to have the best
medicine available — which is you."

We found Mama Leslie weeping on the front porch. I went
into Papa Leslie's room. He was lying in bed, gasping for
breath. The white stubble on his drawn face made him appear
gaunt. It seemed he had aged ten years in three days.

"Baby, you're here!" he whispered, reaching out to hug
me. Then, forcing a wry little smile, he said, "It isn't
everybody who has a movie star to visit them when they're
sick. I'm mighty proud of you. But I told you you'd be
famous someday, didn't I?"

"You've told me a thousand times, and I love you dearly
for it."

My eyes filled. I turned away on the pretext of looking to
see where Mama Leslie was. Papa Leslie coughed and almost
strangled.

"It's this congestion," he said, clutching the neck of his
nightshirt. "Sometimes it's real bad, Baby."

That night, I had a hard time getting off to sleep. The air
seemed heavy and hard to breathe — a sympathetic response
to Papa Leslie's problem, no doubt.

Why didn't Mr. Stambaugh write? It had been three weeks
since the pageant. Every afternoon, I ran in from the bus and
asked Mother, "Any mail today?" But there was no letter.

My disappointment turned into fear, my fear into frustration, my frustration into anger. Why had Mr. Stambaugh even
mentioned the role to me if he wasn't serious about giving
it to me?

In my defiant mood, I seized upon his parting admonition
for me not to cut my hair. That night when everyone was

asleep, I got up, lit the lamp, and slipped into my parents'
room. Ever so quietly, I crept over to my mother's dresser
(two crates with a board across them, covered with a feed-
sack skirt) and picked up her shears. Viewing my dim image
in the mirror, I snipped off my long tresses.

"There!" I said to myself. "No movie, no long hair."

The next morning, a Saturday, Mr. Banks, the mailman,
tooted his car horn up at the main road. It could mean only
one thing — a letter from Mr. Stambaugh. As I ran toward
the mailbox, I pulled my bobbed hair as if I could somehow
restore it to its original length. "My hair! Why did I cut it?"
I cried.

I got the letter out of the box. It had Mr. Stambaugh's
return address. I tore the envelope open.

> Dear Miss Sauls:
>
> At last, everything is set. We begin shooting
> a week from today, which will be May 3, in
> Cornelia. Please arrive no later than Sunday
> evening.
>
> Don't fret about clothes — bring something
> comfortable. But please don't forget to bring
> that wonderful smile and that long, black hair.
>
> Enclosed is my check to cover transporta-
> tion. We can come to final terms concerning
> salary once you're here.
>
> Looking forward to working with you,
>
> > Sincerely,
> > Ken Stambaugh

I read the letter to Mother and bawled, "It's just like
Aunt Mary said. Whenever opportunity knocks, I blow it!"

"Maybe Mr. Stambaugh'll still use you," Mother said. "Oh,
Mickey, I don't know. I'll call your father and see what
he thinks."

"No, don't call him in from work 'cause he'll be mad.
Besides, he won't care. He's never taken an interest in me
and my acting."

Mother summoned him anyhow and made me read the letter aloud.

"I wanted to be in that movie more than anything in my life!" I said. "But now I can't!"

"You'll be there!" Daddy said.

I stared at him. Had I heard him correctly? I ran and threw my arms around his neck. He grasped my arms and slipped them down off his shoulders.

"You'll be there," he repeated. "I'm going with you."

Daddy had bought an old Chevrolet for fifty dollars on a two-year note. He had been wanting to try it out on a trip, and this was the chance. The crops were all planted, and Earl, Mother, and the others could manage until we got back. Deep inside, I felt that Daddy was, for the first time ever, seeing how much my dreams meant to me, and he wanted to help.

I would be out of school three weeks, and only six weeks remained until graduation. My teachers felt the experience would be valuable, so they excused me. I had been given the female lead in the senior play, and I promised to work on my part while away.

Cornelia was in the northeast corner of the state and we were in the southwest corner. From Davisville to Cornelia was almost three hundred miles. Daddy said it would take all day. Instead of our stopping by Papa Leslie's on the way, he drove me over the day before.

Papa Leslie was sitting in his big chair with one blanket over his shoulders and another over his legs, though it was a warm spring day. I put my arms around him and gently squeezed him. He felt lifeless, like a cloth doll.

"Baby," he said, gesturing with a hand that shook as if with palsy, "I want to tell you somethin'. Come close, 'cause I can't do much more'n whisper."

I knelt and took his hands in mine.

"Baby," he said, "I've been hearin' God callin' me home."

"Oh, don't say that! You're gonna be all right."

"No, Baby. You and me, we've had our little jokes. We like to joke with each other, don't we? But this time, I'm not tellin' a joke. God is callin' me. He's gonna come and take me to heaven, just like he came and took your Uncle Jim. This is our goodby, Baby."

"Then I won't go!" I said, tears gushing down my face. "I won't leave you!"

"Of course you're goin'," he said, managing a faint smile. "You're gonna go and do your best, just like always. You'll make this movin' pitcher and then another and then another. You'll be good. Folks'll like you. You'll see. Now you go on, 'cause I want you to. Do it for me."

He pulled his hands out of mine. "Goodby, Baby."

"I love you," I said, looking into his beautiful blue eyes. I walked to the door, then ran out of the house, my heart bursting. As we drove away, I looked back at the house and convulsed with sobs. Daddy just let me cry.

"I'm gonna work real hard, Daddy. I'm gonna do it for Papa Leslie."

My father reached over and put his hand on my knee and kept it there a minute or two.

"You will," he said. "I know you will."

The evening of the next day, after we had checked into the hotel, we were directed to Mr. Stambaugh's room, which doubled as an office.

When he answered our knock, he just stood and stared.

"Don't you recognize me? I'm Mickey Sauls."

"Oh, yes, Mickey. But whatever happened to your hair?"

"Please don't tell me you can't use me. My daddy and I have driven 276 miles to get here."

"Listen," he said, "I need you as much as you need me. We start shooting tomorrow morning, you know. I'm just turning over in my mind some of the changes we'll have to make — description, personality, things like that. No, you've got the part!"

"Thank goodness," I said. Daddy grinned.

The life of a movie star was delicious. Neither Daddy nor I had ever stayed in a hotel before, and we relished ordering whatever we liked from the menu and just signing the check over to the movie company.

The first day on location, Ken (Mr. Stambaugh) watched Daddy rolling a cigarette with one hand, pulling the strings of his Bull Durham sack shut with his teeth. Ken wanted to try it for himself. He failed miserably.

That night, a bellboy knocked on Daddy's door and handed him a carton of Chesterfields with a note: "Mr. Sauls, you're on vacation, remember? Don't spoil it with all that work rolling your own."

The few times Daddy had indulged in store-bought cigarettes, it had been a nickel's worth out of a broken pack at a penny apiece. This was the first full carton of ready-rolls he had ever owned.

My days were long and strenuous. *Rendezvous with Death* depended more upon action than characterization. Ken himself played the lead — a moonshiner harassed by the sheriff. As I remember, the most exciting scene was one in which Ken, to elude the law, hung out over a gorge while clinging to a tree root. The young man who played opposite me was Jack, a singer and a college student. We hit it off fine.

On Tuesday of the third week, Ken announced that he hoped to wind up the shooting on Friday. During the lunch break, Daddy received a telegram.

COME HOME AT ONCE STOP PAPA LOW
AND ASKING FOR MICKEY

At Ken's urgent request, we stayed the rest of the day to film the scenes in which I was essential.

When Daddy and I got to Papa Leslie's, the whole family was there. Mama Leslie came out of his room. "He's kept mumblin' that he wanted to see his baby one more time," she said.

I went in, knelt beside his bed, and grasped his hand.

"Baby," he whispered, "thank God you got here." He wanted to say something else but the effort was too great.

"Don't try to talk, Papa Leslie," I said. "I'm going to stay right here."

He smiled faintly and gave my hand a little squeeze.

I remained there, holding his hand in mine. Within half an hour, Papa Leslie died. A large part of me died with him.

I had resented God's letting Papa Leslie suffer, but now I was strangely able to accept his passing. I thanked God for letting the tired old man slip away peacefully.

God had done some wonderful things for me, but none of his other gifts would compare with this great gift — my dear Papa Leslie.

I missed my Papa Leslie very much, but fortunately I was caught up in a whirl of activity which kept me from sinking into total depression. In school, there was a lot of reading to be done. Then there was the senior play and its demands. Work on the farm had piled up while Daddy and I were away. Also, I went to see Mama Leslie every opportunity I got.

Before I participated in the Miss Georgia pageant and was involved in the movie, I had never given college a serious thought. I assumed that if you had a natural bent for acting, were willing to learn your lines, and really threw yourself into your work — well, that was all there was to it. Associating with college students and college graduates at Warm Springs and at Cornelia, however, made me aware of the advantages college provides an entertainer — or anyone else, for that matter.

A week before school was out, there was a "College Day," with representatives from half a dozen state and private institutions present. Our homeroom teacher had asked which of us would be interested in hearing about the schools, their programs, scholarships, and so forth. I held up my hand.

"Why are you raising your hand?" Grace Mozeley sneered. "You don't have to have a college education to grow collard greens."

"Yeah," one of her chums said. "Besides, you won't have time to go to college, you'll be so busy being a big movie star."

"That'll be enough of that!" the teacher said. "Mickey *are* you seriously interested in college?" The doubt in her voice embarrassed me more than had the cuts from my classmates.

"Yes ma'am."

The class snickered. To them, I was nothing but a share-cropper's daughter. I jumped up and faced them defiantly. "I'm going to college! You just wait and see!"

"I hope that you *can* go, Mickey," the teacher said. "I'd like to see every one of you go. . . . Now, let me see that show of hands again."

At lunchtime, I asked the teacher what was involved in getting a scholarship. Good grades were important, she said, but some colleges paid considerable attention to need.

When the representatives spoke to us, the college that I was most impressed with was Castleberry, which was repre-sented by a recent graduate, a poised young woman from Davisville who pinch-hit for the director of admissions. What captured me was a phrase she read from a printed folder: "A Christian college for women." *They would understand my desperate situation!* I went up to the lady and told her I wanted to go to Castleberry and asked if she would get the college to send me some literature and an application. She said she would.

On the school bus, I let my fancy soar. In addition to my undeniable need, I would win a scholarship on the basis of my acting ability. I could be in plays and even help to direct campus dramatic productions. If they had a farm, I'd work on it if I had to. Earl was working his way through agricul-tural college doing that. Papa Leslie had said I'd be a movie star, and college would be a big step in that direction. College was just another chapter in God's plan for my life.

When I got home, I told Mother about my hopes of winning a scholarship and going to college.

"Mickey, I don't want you getting your hopes up. I'm afraid you'll be disappointed."

I didn't let her skepticism deter me. After all, what did she know about colleges and scholarships?

That night, when I told Daddy my new aspirations, he reacted scornfully. "Just who do you think you are? And what do you propose to use for money — green leaves off the trees?" And to Mother, he said, "Annie Will, we've raised a bigger idiot than I'd ever suspected."

I felt crushed. I thought that at last Daddy understood my ambition. I explained about scholarships.

"Mickey, you're just settin' yourself up for a fall. Take it from me — somebody with experience. You don't get somethin' for nothin'. I don't think you're gonna find any college that's gonna give you a free ride."

"Well, we wouldn't expect 'em to give me four years of education *absolutely free*, would we? I mean, surely you could pay somethin', couldn't you?"

"Mickey, that's the easiest — and hardest — question I've ever answered. I can tell you exactly how much I can pay — zero. So let's forget about it!"

But I couldn't forget about it. I was going to graduate in one week. I would spend part of the summer making personal appearances promoting the movie. Then what would I do? Likely, I would hoe corn and chop cotton until I married. Then I would raise young'uns and help my husband to feed our brood's hungry mouths. The prospect was too dismal for me to contemplate.

The next evening, Mother and I cooked a meal that Daddy would especially like. After eating, he sat down in his rocking chair, tapped out one of the Chesterfields that Ken Stambaugh had given him, and lighted up.

"Daddy, I've been thinking," I said. "I've got twenty-seven dollars saved out of my movie money, and I'll get fifteen dollars a week when I begin doin' personal appearances. By fall, I ought to have almost a hundred dollars saved. That might get me started in college. Do you think you could take a hundred out of this fall's crop to run me 'til Christmas? By then, I'm sure the professors would want to keep me in school and would give me a scholarship. Maybe I could get a job in the dinin' room."

Daddy looked at me real stern. He didn't speak, but "no" was written all over his face.

"But don't you see?" I begged. "I need you to help me. At least talk with me about it."

"Didn't I tell you in plain English I didn't want to hear any more about college? Now leave it be before I take my belt to you."

I slunk off to bed. How I missed Papa Leslie. He always understood me. If I only had him to confide in. Papa Leslie — he would say to me, "Baby, *pray* about it."

Dear Lord, I know you want me to amount to somethin'. But how can I be somebody if I don't have the education? That'd be as impossible as a farmer farmin' without a plow. Please open up the way for me to go to college.

The very next day, a Saturday, the director of admissions of Castleberry College presented himself at our door. He couldn't have picked a worse day. Our pig was rooting around the front steps. Mother came to the door in a stylish dress which Aunt Mary had outgrown. Its inappropriateness as a house dress made her appear ludicrous. I was in the back yard boiling clothes. I was ashamed to come around front when Mother called me. Dirty little faces peeked around the side of the house.

The director was visibly shaken but attempted to maintain his decorum.

"Miss Sauls, I've come to speak with you about your interest in attending Castleberry College. Tell me something about yourself."

"Please sit down," I said, motioning to the porch swing.

For perhaps fifteen minutes, I described my schooling and my experience as an entertainer and actress, and he told me about the college.

"I've just got to go to college," I said. "I'll wait on tables, scrub floors, anything."

Mother, who had been listening from inside the house, came out and said, "I hope you'll give her a chance. I'll help any way I can. Maybe we could send the college ham, eggs, butter, potatoes — things like that. We'd pay you somehow."

"Well, Miss Sauls, you seem to be a likely candidate," he said. "Here's an application form for admission and one for seeking a grant-in-aid. Perhaps we would be able to arrange a modest scholarship for you, although it's really quite late and most of what desperately little money we had is gone. How much would your parents be able to pay down in the event you are accepted?"

"Well, sir, I have twenty-seven dollars and I'll earn some more this summer. Would that be enough?"

"And how much will your father pay down?"

"He — he wouldn't be able to pay anything — not anything."

The gentleman cleared his throat. He put the descriptive folder which he'd said he would leave with me back into his briefcase.

"I'm sorry, Miss Sauls, but I've wasted my time and yours. Your situation is quite impossible. You see, without money, we cannot operate either."

"But mister! You don't understand! I've *got* to go to college! I'm not too proud to work like a dog — in the fields, if necessary, like my brother does at agricultural college."

"I'm sorry, Miss Sauls." A tip of the hat and he was gone.

Stunned, I stood and watched his car turn into the big road. Every revolution of the wheels took my chance for a college education further from me. I ran to Mother. She wrapped her arms around me.

"They call it a *Christian* college," I sobbed. "Well, what's so Christian about it?"

A little before noon, Ida came by to see if I could ride into Davisville with her and her father. I got Daddy's permission and quickly dressed.

Ida had assumed I was going to the movies with her, but as we walked toward the theater, I told her I wanted to see if I could borrow some money for college.

The first person I called upon was the banker on whose place we had formerly lived. He was very kind, but he said the only way he could lend me money was for my father to go on a note with me. I told him Daddy wouldn't do that.

I had heard our principal say that he had borrowed most of his college money from a local lawyer. But when I visited the lawyer's office and stated my need, he said he didn't believe in women going to college. "Their place is in the home."

My last call was on the well-to-do owner of a dry goods store. I told him about my acting ability and how hard I had worked on the farm — how much cotton I could pick in a day, and so forth. I would pay him back with interest.

"If this were 1928, I'd be able to help you, Mickey," he said, "but it's not. It's 1935. With this Depression, nobody has any money to give away or loan. I'm sorry."

That night, I did no more than tease the food on my plate. Daddy went to the barn to doctor a sick calf, and I started helping Mother with the dishes.

"I know you're disappointed over not gettin' to go to college," she said. "But, Mickey, we're just pore folks. You might as well ask your daddy to take you to the moon as to send you to college. And even if we could scrape the money together somehow, it wouldn't be fair to your sisters — you'd be takin' clothes off their backs and vittles off their plates. Just be thankful that we have a roof over our heads and enough food to get by on. Some people aren't that lucky."

"Thankful" for a shack with a leaky roof? "Thankful" for cornbread and peas? "Lucky"? If I'm "lucky," I'd like to see what "unlucky" looks like!

9

back to route 2, davisville, georgia

I graduated the first week in June, and the next week *Rendezvous with Death* premiered in Cornelia. Ken Stambaugh arranged for several of us principals to be there. During the next few weeks, as the film opened in a dozen or so Georgia cities and towns, we made guest appearances. Our presence was supposed to turn each opening into an event. Sometimes it did; sometimes it didn't.

I enjoyed the tour immensely. I liked meeting people, talking to folks in the entertainment field, staying in hotels, eating in restaurants. To be honest, I liked the attention. I hoped that the publicity I received might snatch me from a fate which I considered worse than death: returning to my daddy's farm and working in the fields. But when the touring had ended, back to the farm I went. Being a high school graduate made it worse. "High school graduate" sounds a bit hollow to many people nowadays, but in 1935 it wasn't something to sneeze at. Half my classmates had dropped out between first grade and graduation.

But what difference did *my* diploma make? Not a bit. I did the same hard labor, worked the same interminable hours, and faced the same bleak future as before.

I lost my pride. I didn't care about my dress or grooming, and I let my shoulders slump. I grew lazy in my speech. I junked my movie magazines. There was nothing – and no-body – to inspire and encourage me. Many nights, bored stiff, I went to bed shortly after supper. Often, I cried myself to sleep.

My religious life declined. Strangely, my slump came just as my father's zeal perked up. As a boy, Daddy went to Sunday School and church, as did his fourteen brothers and sisters. Grandma Sauls was a veteran children's teacher. But in his later youth and early adulthood, Daddy saw himself as a nobody in the church – he didn't have decent clothes and he had no money to spare – so he quit attending.

The Sauls were great singers, and when I was twelve or so, Daddy – with his brothers Russell and Doc and his cousin Bright – formed a quartet, with Aunt Millie as their pianist. They were in great demand for services, singings, and socials. When they sang "Jesus Paid It All" and "The Old Rugged Cross," their harmony was the sweetest music I'd ever heard – except for Papa Leslie's fiddle playing, of course.

Feeling himself appreciated, Daddy began attending church regularly, and he insisted that the whole family go. He had Mother buy Sunday clothes for the boys and nice material for the girls' Sunday dresses, while he himself purchased a suit. As a fervent little Christian, I had been proud to go to church with my daddy, but now – doubting whether God really cared about me – I hated being forced to go.

Occasionally I wrote to Aunt Mary, and my blues must have shown, because when she made her vacation visit to Mama Leslie's, she came over to our house and proposed that I go to Atlanta to live with her and attend business school. Aunt Mary was now divorced, and she needed me to help look after her little daughter, Legene. In turn, she would pay my tuition, buy my books, and give me some spending money.

I said I really didn't want to go to business school, which was true. But my primary concern was that Aunt Mary and I wouldn't get along. Although we loved each other, our temperaments clashed. However, the more I thought about spending the fall and winter on the farm, the more I warmed to Aunt Mary's proposition.

Although Daddy wasn't an admirer of Aunt Mary's, he recognized that she had pulled herself up by her bootstraps, as it were, and he respected her for it. Also, he saw I was terribly despondent and he thought Aunt Mary's rollicking humor and fiery determination might be good for me. He hated to lose my helping hands, but I suspect he viewed my griping to be a threat to the family's morale and commitment to hard work. So he said I could go if I wanted to.

Aunt Mary clinched my decision. "If you want anything out of life, you've got to go after it!" she declared. I knew she was right. Nothing good was going to come and hunt me up on the farm.

"I'd like to come, Aunt Mary," I said enthusiastically.

"Good. I'll pick you up Sunday at two o'clock."

Life in Atlanta was different, although I still faced "chores." I came in from business school and looked after Legene until Aunt Mary got home. I started supper, and after supper saw that Legene got her bath and went to bed. I also did the breakfast dishes. It was a lot of work, though not heavy. Still, my room and board was worth it — especially when I considered the alternative.

Legene was a spoiled child. As soon as the novelty of having me around wore off, she went to all lengths to provoke me. Her favorite trick was hiding. Sometimes I would spend half an hour looking for her, scared stiff that Aunt Mary would arrive to find her missing and decide to send me home.

One day I searched the house, looked in a nearby grocery store, and checked with neighbors, but Legene was nowhere to be found. When Aunt Mary came, I was scared speechless. I finally got it out that Legene was missing.

"Missing?" Aunt Mary bellowed. "For heaven sakes, Mickey, can't you keep up with her? After all, that's your responsibility when I'm not here."

"I'm sorry, Aunt Mary. I even thought about calling the

police but figured I ought to wait until you got home."

A tapping sound drew our attention to a window at the head of the stairs. Outside, astraddle a tree limb, was Legene, waving to us and beaming triumphantly.

When she came in, she said, "Mother, you should have seen Mickey going everywhere looking for me! She was *so* funny!"

Aunt Mary laughed. "Honey, you shouldn't play jokes on Mickey like that!"

"But she was *so* fun-ny!"

"It wasn't funny to *me*, Legene," I protested.

"Now, now, Mickey, you mustn't take things so seriously," Aunt Mary said.

I learned that the way to handle Legene was to give her a licking; then, when she complained to Aunt Mary, I would deny ever hitting her.

In business school, I quickly mastered typing and shorthand, although I wasn't truly motivated. Spelling and business English required some homework but presented no real problem. Even with my time-consuming chores, I had a good bit of time to use as I pleased, especially on weekends.

I rejoiced in Atlanta's educational and cultural opportunities. There were lectures, museums, and concerts. After a couple of months, the school placed me in a part-time job in an insurance office, and the pay enabled me to take dancing lessons. I learned about grooming and dress through observation, and the cosmetics company consultants who periodically gave demonstrations in the department stores must have said to themselves, "Here *she* comes again!"

I learned a wonderful thing about Atlanta — the city was in love with beautiful girls. Many of the men, young and old alike, spent part of their lunch hour standing on Peachtree Street watching the girls go by. Every few weeks, some organization had a pageant to select a Miss Whatever, and I added half a dozen cups to my trophy collection. One of them was a handsome cup I won as second runner-up in the Miss Atlanta contest.

But the most enjoyable part of my stay in Atlanta was

being able to go to the movies once or twice a week. Not only did I see new releases, but also some of the celebrated older ones that I had missed.

By 1935, the studios had crawled out of the financial abyss into which they had tumbled in 1932-33. One of the devices that rescued them was the star system. Since film production costs had risen sharply and remained fairly constant, the film companies expanded box office receipts by packing half a dozen stars into a single film: *Grand Hotel* — Garbo, the Barrymores, Beery, Hersholt, Stone, and my favorite, Joan Crawford. *Dinner at Eight* — Harlow, John Barrymore, Beery, Dressler, Burke. *Night Flight* — Gable, Montgomery, Loy, the Barrymores, and Helen Hayes. I caught up with several Crawford pictures — *Rain; Today We Live; Chained;* and (released that year) *Forsaking All Others,* with Gable and Montgomery. Star-struck girl that I was, I felt I was getting an awful lot for my money.

Nearly every month, some big names came into town for a personal appearance in connection with their films. Usually the performer would do a song, dance, or monologue; or, several members of a cast might present a "piece" of the movie. Afterward, I was always among the crowd clamoring for autographs.

In that era, everyone talked movies just as they talk television today, so I was never at a loss for conversational material. There were more than 500 official fan clubs, with a membership of 750,000, and I was proud that my name had helped to boost Joan Crawford, Clark Gable, and Jean Harlow to the pinnacle.

I had money for movie magazines, which I devoured. Reading one of them, I came upon a bit of information that caused my ambition to soar. Ginger Rogers, like Joan Crawford, had become a star via the Charleston route. As a rural Texas girl, she had learned the Charleston and other styles of dancing without any special training. ("I just watched and did what everybody else was doing.") Her ambition was to become an English teacher, and in her pursuit of a college education, she went to Dallas for the state Charleston contest. She won, and the rest is movie history. Her story perked me up. If she could make it without a college education, I could!

These days in Atlanta were the happiest days of my life up to that time — and then it happened: I was graduated. My reason for living with Aunt Mary vanished — anyhow, I had imposed on her long enough.

I received a diploma in secretarial sciences — a diploma I never intended to use. I didn't want a business career; I wanted to go to Hollywood! I was afraid that if I took an office position, I would fall into the security trap and let my ambition for an acting career die.

I couldn't find a decent job in entertainment that would pay my board, and I didn't want a business job, so I did the only thing I knew to do: I went back home to the farm.

My bus arrived in Davisville in the late afternoon, and Daddy and Bobbie met me. As we drove past the school and through the shadow of the infamous persimmon tree, I thought of the good times spent playing ball with the boys and the bad times being humiliated by the girls.

"Daddy, whatever happened to Grace Mozely?"

"She married Durwood Johnston. He works at the planin' mill. They have a baby girl."

I was surprised to find myself wanting the best for Grace. My lack of resentment made me feel unreal. I searched my heart, but sure enough, I found no malice.

We also passed the little Methodist church that we kids looked after — the church where I had "made a spectacle" of myself. I decided I would attend services there some Sunday.

When we got home, Mother and my sisters rushed out to greet me. I saw in my mother's face the rigors of birthing children and working in the fields, but how good to have her squeeze me and to know we would have time to talk, woman to woman. Each excited child, in turn, came up and hugged me.

"After you've rested," Bobbie said, "I'll show you where

we buried Trouble. We can pick some flowers, put them in this pretty jar that I saved, and put them on his grave."

Mother must have had every pot and pan she owned on the old wood stove. I identified the aromas of cornbread, sweet potatoes, and turnip greens.

"I've cut up two fryers and as soon as I get them cooked, we'll eat," Mother said.

When we sat down, Daddy repeated his familiar grace: "Oh, Lord, give us thankful hearts for these and all other blessin's." But he delayed the usual "Amen" and inserted: "And thank you, Lord, for bringin' Mickey home safe and sound."

The family had replaced the old coal-oil lamp with an Aladdin lamp, which was, Daddy boasted, "the next thing to an electric light bulb."

"But it doesn't draw snakes as good," Mary chimed in.

After supper, Daddy fetched a bushel of seed potatoes from the crib. We sat in a semicircle in the glow of the fire, built to take the chill off the early spring evening, and cut the potatoes into sections. There are some things you never forget: Two pieces out of the small ones, three or four out of the big ones — and each piece must have a good eye.

My sisters hung onto my every word about Atlanta, for none of them had been there. And I, in turn, enjoyed hearing of family friends and neighbors.

For my homecoming, Daddy had bought a second-hand bed for me. Angel asked if she could sleep with me, and I said yes. That night I wished that — for just one more time — I could again sleep four deep with my brother and sisters.

The next morning, Daddy let me sleep until breakfast. I was surprised to have slept through the clanging bell.

After breakfast, Daddy hitched up one of his mules — he now had two — and plowed several rows for the potatoes in the garden. The soil smelled fresh and good. As I moved along the furrows, carefully spotting the potato chunks eye-side-up, two robins bounced along in front of me picking up earthworms.

A wave of nostalgia swept over me. I wanted to ask my daddy to stop and sing "Old Grizzly Bear," but didn't. However, I did indulge one impulse:

"Daddy, late this afternoon, could we go fishing?"

"I don't know of anything to stop us," he said. And we went.

I don't want to suggest that my return to the farm continued to be blissful. It didn't. The sun was just as scorching, the dust just as choking, and the work just as backbreaking as before. Occasionally, my sisters became obnoxious. And my parents clashed with me over my assertions of independence and my "newfangled" ideas about race relations, political reforms, and individual freedom.

But during the first few days, heaven for me was Route 2, Davisville, Georgia. Where earlier there had been bitter resignation, I now found joy, and where there had been resentment and denial, there now was acceptance.

I sensed why this was so. The stomach-rumbling deprivation, the harsh demands laid upon us by my father, the lack of opportunity to engage in broadening conversation — these circumstances had been hard to accept. But now, having returned to them voluntarily, I was no longer at war with them. I could even appreciate what I had become because of — and in spite of — them.

I would be home for just a little while, I told myself, because I was destined to greater and grander things. But *someday*, when I became *somebody*, I sensed that I would look back upon my days on the farm and cherish what they had contributed to my life.

10

mickey sauls, traveling director

On her visits, Aunt Mary always brought me old newspapers and magazines. In one paper, I found an appealing classified ad: "Wanted, girls with flair for dramatics. Exciting and profitable career awaits you. . . ." I wrote, and several days later I received a letter and printed folder.

I had feared this might be a sleazy modeling agency; instead, it sounded like a legitimate enterprise. A production company in Atlanta trained girls and then sent them out to direct plays under local sponsorship (schools, churches, civic organizations) using local talent. It seemed right up my alley, except for one thing: fifteen dollars a week for instruction and room and board. For six weeks, that would be ninety dollars! I wrote to the manager, a Mr. Henry Phillips, and he agreed to let me put down forty dollars, which I had saved, and pay the remainder later out of my commissions.

I was thrilled over the prospect. Heightening my anticipation was the fact that a young man from Davisville, Ollie Jordan, was attending school in Atlanta. During the period following my return to the farm, Saturday night dates with blond, blue-eyed Ollie (who came home in his car every weekend) had been the thing that kept me going.

From our school days, Ollie remembered little about me other than my name. I, on the other hand, knew all about him. The Jordans lived in a big, white house with a nice, green lawn. (Most folks had bare front yards that they swept clean with a brush broom.) A windmill provided the main house and barn with running water, and a Delco generator produced electricity. To me, who had moved half a dozen times, the most incredible thing was the fact that Ollie had lived in this one house all his life!

When Ollie first asked me for a date, I accepted, thinking that going out with him would be a pleasant novelty. He was good looking and he had a car and plenty of spending money. I didn't think he could ever be serious with me — and I didn't want to be serious with him — or anyone else, for that matter. I didn't want a marriage to sidetrack my ambition to become a movie star.

As we dated more, I found myself growing fonder of Ollie, and he seemed to care for me. I felt insecure. I didn't want to be tied down, yet I couldn't bring myself to give him up — indeed, I worried for fear he wouldn't be able to see my merits and aspirations for my squalid circumstances. But if I moved to Atlanta and took employment — well, I would no longer be a poor country girl.

The train started to roll, and I waved final goodbys to my family. When all familiar landmarks had passed from view, I got up and stretched. I tried to affect the nonchalance of a much-traveled lady with business matters on her mind. However, the rumble, roar, and sway were more than I had anticipated, and I'm sure that my alarm over our careening around curves showed through my facade.

Later, I went back to eat. I had eaten in Atlanta cafeterias and coffee shops, but they didn't compare in elegance with the service of the dining car. As I sat at my linen-covered table, I said to myself, "Miss Mickey Sauls, traveling director, it's a fantastic life you'll be leading."

When I lugged my things off at the Terminal Station in Atlanta, I wondered if I would recognize Mr. Phillips. But there was one person on the platform who *had* to be him; a handsome man in a gray pin stripe, wearing a red tie and red carnation. He rocked up on tiptoes and waved, then rushed over and said, "You're Mickey!" He asked if he might take me to lunch. When I said I had already eaten, he suggested, "Well, why don't we get right on out to the Training Center?" The center was a large stone building in a retreat setting — eighteen miles from the city, actually. The isolation, the folder said, permitted concentrated study.

Ollie had planned to come and see me, but then I learned that no visitors were permitted. Maybe it was just as well. Still, I was already missing Ollie more than I thought I would. I was pleased when girls who saw his photo called him handsome.

For six weeks, we talked, ate, and slept dramatics. As a special project, each of us was given a play. We had to memorize all the lines, be able to play all the parts, make announcements, change the scenes — everything. At graduation, we were to do all this in front of our classmates and instructors. Some of the other girls spoke of it as an ordeal; for me, it was an exciting challenge.

On graduation eve, I was in my room running over my lines when a girl stopped by and whispered that Ollie had sent word through one of the cooks that he was waiting for me in his car just outside the gate. I didn't want to jeopardize graduation, but neither did I want to jeopardize my relationship with Ollie. Besides, I was terribly hungry to see him. So I sneaked out.

It was good to feel Ollie's arms again. I told him I had only ten minutes, and although we talked in rapid-fire order, the time flew and I had to say goodby. I slipped back in without being noticed.

The next day, my presentation went without a hitch and I was graded A-plus. Mr. Phillips congratulated me and told me I would go on the road the following week. Meanwhile, costumes, props, literature, and posters were being shipped to my first town. A booking agent arranged our engagements with an eye to keeping distances between towns as short as possible. Usually, he scheduled our productions two weeks apart—which made for concentrated effort.

For six months, I traveled throughout Georgia, South Carolina, and Alabama. I stayed in hotels, boarding houses, and private rooms, and I met many interesting people. (Occasionally, Ollie showed up, which was a delightful bonus.) I loved the work, and I thrived on the attention. In those days before television, local productions were celebrated events, and the lady who directed them was regarded as special. I must have advised a hundred young people concerning careers in dramatics. My plays were invariably successful, which meant that the sponsor made money, my company made money, and I made money — which kept everybody happy. I cleared up my indebtedness the first six weeks.

The engagement that stands out in my memory — and for obvious reasons — was in a north Alabama town. A sweet little old lady called "Miss Tissa" met the train and walked me to her house, where I was to stay. It was an antebellum house, complete with big, white columns. It was quaintly furnished with period furniture and heirloom bric-a-brac and objects of art. The furnishings blended with Miss Tissa's conversation, which ran heavily to talk of the United Daughters of the Confederacy.

The house was only two blocks from the school, where the play was to be presented, and four blocks from downtown. The local movie theater was heavily promoting Janet Gaynor in *A Star Is Born*, which was to be presented the same Thursday and Friday nights as my own production. I knew that the picture, which had been released only a few weeks earlier, would cut into my attendance — in fact, I myself was dying to see it. (A later version starring Judy Garland was released in 1954.)

We had a good audience Thursday night, but Friday — one of those cold, drizzling nights when you'd rather stay home — was a bust. It was my first financial disaster. I rushed the performance, cut short the curtain calls, and threw my properties into the trunk, tagging it for the next town. Then one of the actors dropped me off at the movie theater just as the second showing began.

It was uncanny. Janet Gaynor was me! She was a talented young woman just waiting to be discovered—and Frederic March attended to that! If she could become a star, why couldn't I? I had to go to Hollywood. Right then! That night!

I left the theater and ran down the street, oblivious to the rain. I pounded on Miss Tissa's door.

"Why, honey, you're sopping wet," she said. "Come in here and dry that dress by the fire. Tell me about tonight. I don't guess you had as good a crowd as we had last night."

"It was pretty dismal," I said absently. Then I blurted it out: "Miss Tissa, I'm going to Hollywood!"

"Hollywood? My, my! You said you were going to Luthersville, up on the mountain, and now they're sending you to Hollywood?"

"No, Miss Tissa, *they're* not sending me. I'm quitting. I'm going to Hollywood on my own."

"You going to put on plays out there?"

"No, ma'am, I'm going to be a movie star."

"Well, if you can act like you can put on plays, you'll be a success, I'll tell you that!"

"Thanks. Is there a train out of here going west tonight?"

"No, but a train to Nashville, Tennessee, comes through at eleven-thirty."

"Good. I'll catch it. I can transfer in Nashville."

"You could except it doesn't stop at our depot any more!"

"Oh, heck! I've *got* to get off to Hollywood tonight!"

"Why tonight, honey? Get a good night's rest and go tomorrow."

"If I wait till tomorrow, I might talk myself out of it."

"Back when I was teaching at Agricola and we wanted to catch the train at night, we built a fire on the tracks."

"Are you suggesting we do that?"

"Well, I don't see why not. I've got some kindling wood we could use. I'll get it while you change clothes and pack."

In spite of my protests that she might catch her death of cold, Miss Tissa slogged to the depot with me. Under the protection of the eaves, she got several sticks blazing and soon had a fire going on the tracks.

I figured the engineer would run right through our signal and ball it on down the line, but he didn't. He brought the train to a squealing halt. The conductor stepped down, expressed consternation, and hurried me aboard.

"Miss Tissa, don't forget to change that tag on the trunk so those costumes will go back to the company. And don't you catch cold. Goodby, and thanks!"

"God bless you, child."

The conductor grumbled over having to write me a ticket, and the passengers grumbled over being awakened. They had their things spread out, leaving me nowhere to sit. I went into the lounge and began drying my hair over a vent. I dozed off to be awakened by the conductor calling, "Nash-ville — Nash-ville, Tennessee!"

As I got off, I saw that the rain had shrunk my cheap crepe dress, which was now three inches above my petticoat, leaving my knees showing. I walked into the waiting room holding my suitcase in one hand and trying to smooth down my dress with the other. I drew whistles from men and snorts from women.

In the rest room, I was confronted by stalls with locks which demanded a dime in the slot. I had no dime, but I wasn't about to parade through that waiting room again to get change, so I crawled under one of the doors, soiling my abbreviated skirt in the process.

I went to a ticket window and asked for a ticket to Hollywood, California. When the man told me how much it would be, I realized I didn't have enough money.

"Is there anyone who might wire you money?"

"No."

"How old are you?"

"That's a right personal question."

"I'm not being fresh. I want to help you. You'll have to say how old you are."

"Nineteen."

"Then you're still a minor. Hmmm. See that lady over there at the desk? Maybe she can help you."

The woman smiled and said, "I'm the lady people tell their troubles to. We're the Travelers Aid Society, don't you know?" She pointed to the lettering on a lighted globe above her desk. "Now tell me what's on your mind. By the way, how old are you?"

"I'm nineteen."

"Then you're still a minor."

"I know."

"Well, anyway, what can I do for you?"

"I'm on my way to Hollywood, California, and I don't have enough money for my ticket."

"Why don't you?"

"I — I had it, but I lost it. I lost a ten-dollar bill, so I'm short. Can you help me? You do help people to get where they're going, don't you?"

"That all depends on where they're going and why. Do your parents know where you are and where you are going?"

"No ma'am."

"But they *have* to know, dear. You're a *minor*."

"I may be a minor, as you say, but I've been out earning my own living and. . ."

"Yes, I can see that," the lady said, eying my short skirt.

"I'm not running away, not from my parents or the police or anybody else. But you aren't going to help me — you're just going to pry into my personal affairs." I started to go.

"No, wait a minute," she said. "We can give you clothes — or food. We just aren't permitted to give anyone money."

"And money is all I need," I said, striding away.

"Wait, Miss —. What *is* your name?" She was running alongside me as though she would lose her job if I got away. Without thinking, I blurted out, "My name is Mickey Sauls and I'm from Davisville, Georgia, and if you want to know anything else, come to see me in Hollywood, California."

I ducked out the front door and ran down the street. At that moment, a Greyhound bus rolled by. *That's it, the bus! Buses are cheaper. I'll catch a bus to Hollywood!*

11

learning about life, and god, the hard way

Three days later, I was in Hollywood! When I stepped off the bus, my back and legs felt as though I had walked the more than two thousand miles. I thought that if I ever saw another hamburger, I would die. But my mind's focus was on the future, not the past. In a few minutes, I would break my last dollar to catch a transit bus out to Hollywood. There, another star would be born. I was an unknown on her way to becoming a known.

I was already better known than I wanted to be, it turned out. I had no more than stepped off the bus when a policewoman addressed me.

"Miss Sauls?"

"Yes."

"I'm Officer Burke of the Los Angeles Police Department. This is Mrs. Cook of the Welfare Department. We have a protective custody order on you. Would you please come with us?"

"You're the police? Am I being arrested? I haven't done anything wrong, honest."

"Why don't we talk about your situation over coffee and a doughnut?" Mrs. Cook suggested.

"I know! It's the Travelers Aid Society, isn't it?"

"Well, yes," said Officer Burke. "It was through them that we heard about you."

"You make me sound like a criminal. I've told you, I haven't done anything wrong. And I don't want any coffee and doughnuts — I just want to be left alone. I have my rights!"

"As a minor, your rights are somewhat circumscribed," Mrs. Cook said. "But let's not create a scene out here in front of everybody. It won't hurt you to come in and sit down and talk this over, will it?"

Grudgingly, I went into the coffee shop and sat down. Purely to be contrary, I ordered orange juice and apple pie.

"Miss Sauls, I must ask you some personal questions," Mrs. Cook said. "First, how much money do you have with you? Second, do you have employment? And third, have you a place to stay?"

"As to money, I've got some, all right. As to a job, I'm an experienced drama director, and a drama director can find employment any time she chooses. What was the other question?"

"Do you have a place to stay?"

"Well, you've got hotels out here, haven't you?"

"Miss Sauls," Officer Burke said firmly, "would you please open your purse and show us what money you have?"

"No. You have no right!"

"Miss Sauls," Mrs. Cook implored, "you are in our custody by court order. Please cooperate with us. We don't want to cause you any undue trouble."

"Okay, I admit I've got only a dollar and fifteen cents. But is that a crime?"

"It's not a crime, no," Mrs. Cook said. "However, it is a concern of the court. You are a young woman under age 21 — a minor — and you have no place to stay and no visible means of support."

"May we have your parents' name and address?" Officer Burke asked. "We have your name, Mickey Sauls, and we know you're from some little place in Georgia."

"I'm not telling you another thing!"

"Martha, we aren't getting anywhere with her. Why don't I just carry her on out to the center?"

"Okay," Mrs. Cook said, shrugging. "Don't say I didn't try."

I was escorted to a patrol car. "Would you prefer to sit up here with me?" Officer Burke asked.

"No. Since you're treating me like a criminal, why not go all the way?"

She opened a back door, and after I got in, locked it. We were separated by a metal grating and a wall of silence.

The center was a two-story, white brick building. On a plate over the door was the address: "116 So. Hope St." As we entered the barnlike reception area, I was greeted by a chorus of "You won't like it here!" followed by giggling.

I was embarrassed.

"Don't pay any attention to them," Officer Burke said. "Come over here to the housemother's desk."

The housemother wrote down my name when it was given her by the policewoman. When she asked for other information, I refused.

"You won't get anywhere with her right now," Officer Burke said. "Maybe a little time here will bring her around."

"Miss Sauls," the housemother said, speaking in the manner of a tour guide, "this is the county's Home for Women. Women come to us for a variety of reasons. Some have flagrantly violated the law, others have been found in compromising situations, and some lack any visible means of support. Unfortunately, Los Angeles County attracts a very large number of girls and young women who want to seek their fortunes in the movies, or following conventions, or whatever. For the protection of society and their own best interest, we cannot let them loiter. You will have a room, which you will share with another young woman, Mildred Jackson. I'll send for her now, and she will help you get oriented and settled."

"*Settled?* How long will I be here?"

"That depends. One thing it depends upon is your co-operation."

My roommate was a black girl, seventeen years old. She'd been picked up soliciting on the streets, she told me matter-of-factly. I had never shared a room with a black woman before. The fact that she was a prostitute made me feel itchy. As it turned out, Mildred had an abiding sense of loyalty to friends, a deep religious conviction, and a sparkling sense of humor. If it hadn't been for her humor, I might not have made it through the next few days.

The cleaning, cooking, and other services were handled by the residents themselves. My first day, I was assigned to work in the kitchen with seven other women. I didn't mind cooking, but I hated washing those giant pots and pans. When I started dragging out my work, the salaried dietitian came over and said, "You deserve one warning. If you don't do your share of the work, your fellow residents will call you before a kangaroo court, and if they find you guilty, they'll run you through the belt line."

I hustled the rest of that day. That night, Mildred showed me two blue spots on the back of her thigh. "Somebody swung the wrong end of her belt," she said.

Except at night, the doors of the center were not locked. Few girls dared cross the threshhold, however. One girl stepped outside for a smoke and the housemother, who was called "Mother Baskin" by some and "Mother Grump" by others, confined her to her room for three days.

The center was a dreary place, especially on rainy days. That's when I missed Ollie and my family most. The residents were a rough bunch, but a minimum of discipline was needed. Nobody wanted to be hauled into court on a disturbance charge. Living with these women placed some of us under great pressure. One girl went berserk and was hauled away in a straitjacket. Mildred, who talked the language of the streets and was recognized as a scrapper, was my protection.

I was being held incommunicado, but by my own choosing. Mrs. Baskin wouldn't send me before the court to get my situation straightened out until my parents had been contacted, and I wouldn't identify them. In the first place, I didn't want them to know where I was, and, second, I didn't want them to know I was practically in jail.

Several days later, however, I decided that I would never get out of detention unless my parents notified the authorities that it was okay with them for me to proceed to Hollywood. Also, I feared that my parents would try to locate me through the production company, and, failing, become alarmed. So I wrote to Mother, told her my predicament, and asked her to write the center.

One night, a police sweep of gambling places brought half a dozen movie-like molls into our midst. None was charged — again the "compromising circumstances" allegation; they were, nonetheless, real toughies, female hoods who delighted in keeping the center in an uproar. They set fires in wastebaskets, stole personal property, and spread malicious gossip which led to clawing, hair-pulling altercations. Every day, a police car came to haul somebody into court — or to the hospital emergency room.

I just plain didn't like hassles, so I found asylum on the roof. A corner up there became "my" place. The roof, which was fenced in, was used for drying clothes. When I wasn't on duty somewhere, I went up there and sat in my corner on a stool which the shorter girls used for hanging clothes on the line. Usually there was a refreshing breeze, and the solitude gave me a chance to be alone with my thoughts.

One of the ideas that came to me was that we inmates ought not to waste our energies opposing each other; instead, we ought to work together for our common good. I offered this thought during one of the kangaroo courts (which everyone was compelled to attend). I said we might even form prayer chains and pray for each other.

"Prayer, hell!" sneered one of the toughies. "What we need to do is to break out of here!"

"No, I think Mickey has a good idea," Mildred said.

There was a cacophany of pro and con arguments. The

molls huddled and came out with a proposal of their own: Everyone would draw straws, and the two getting short straws would be the "hit" team. The hit team would lure Mother Baskin into the basement, where one of them would hit her with a piece of pipe. With her out of the way, it would be no trouble subduing and tying up Walter, the ancient custodian. Then everyone would escape.

The idea of violence against the housemother was abhorrent to me. Besides, I might find myself as one of the fated pair. I got my imaginative little mind to concocting an alternative, and when I offered it, it won the majority's favor. I called it our "Do-as-You-Please Evening" rather than a "break." Everyone was to return by midnight.

During the next day, Mother Baskin should have suspected trouble. All the residents suddenly became appearance conscious; they were taking showers and washing and rolling their hair. That night as we came into the mess hall for supper, Mother Baskin said proudly, "My, but you girls look nice tonight!"

As we were finishing the meal, I asked Mother Baskin if I could get a jar of preserves, and she said yes. When I returned, I said, "Mother Baskin, there's a shelf that's been sagging and now it's fallen. Some jars of canned food have busted."

"Walter!" Mother Baskin called. "We'd better check the pantry shelves."

Once they were in the pantry, I slammed the door and locked it. The girls ran out of the house, some in pairs and some singly.

I took a bus downtown, where I caught a sightseeing bus to Hollywood. (I had borrowed two dollars from Mildred.) The tall buildings and neon lights of downtown Los Angeles thrilled me. As we motored through hillside clusters of homes — some plain, some pretentious — I suddenly longed to feel the warmth of my own home again.

In Hollywood, I didn't get to see much except the shopping district, which looked like any other such area. The driver pointed out a few homes of stars, but I glimpsed little more than lights far back from the street. About the most exciting thing I saw was the street sign, "Hollywood and Vine." It didn't matter, I said to myself — I would come back in a few days.

We returned to L.A. and I caught a bus to the detention center. When I arrived (at five before twelve), six police cars were out front. I was scared, but I knew that running away would only add to my troubles. As I walked into the reception area, I was confronted by a sea of blue uniforms. There were also officials from the welfare department and juvenile court.

Someone had ratted on me. I was fingered as one of the ringleaders. The police sergeant wanted to take me to jail, but Mother Baskin interceded. "We don't want to turn well-meaning young girls into hardened criminals," she said. "True, it was hot and stuffy in that pantry, but I wasn't hurt. Besides, most of the girls are back now, and I'm sure the others will show up. No, I'd rather just confine Mickey to her room."

She prevailed and all of the group left except for one officer, who stayed the rest of the night.

I recognized that I had concocted something evil. I had anguished an old woman who, it turned out, felt more charitable toward me than I toward her. Although I hadn't given the possibility a thought, she could have suffocated in that pantry. Moreover, some of those women would never return. I should have known that beforehand. I had turned lions out of their cages.

The next morning, I stayed in my room. Mildred brought me breakfast — a cup of coffee and a piece of dry toast.

"I tried to tell them it was my idea, but they wouldn't listen," she said. "I already have a record, so I figured it couldn't hurt me much."

"Thanks, Mildred. You're the most generous person I've ever met."

That afternoon, Mother Baskin found me propped up in bed reading a magazine.

"Mickey," she said, "you're having it too good. You've got to learn your lesson. I'm going to put you on the laundry detail for the next three days."

The laundry detail was considered the worst assignment, primarily because heavy baskets of clothes had to be lugged up four flights of steps to the roof.

"Oh, Mother Baskin!" I said, faking disappointment. "Anything but that!"

"No, Mickey, you get on down there."

Unknowingly, Mother Baskin had thrown Br'er Rabbit into the briar patch. The laundry detail was my favorite assignment because between loads I could sit in my spot on the roof. And since she hadn't said anything about my being confined to my room at night, I could spend my evenings on the roof, too.

In addition to affording me welcome relief from the turbulent life below, the roof provided me with a place to meditate, pray, and – often – cry. It was my "chapel." In retrospect, I feel that I grew immensely as a person – a Christian person – during my time spent on that roof. As the sun set, it cast a warm glow upon the skyline. On clear nights, it seemed that I could reach up and gather a handful of stars, which lifted my spirits; on some darker nights, clouds scudding across the face of the moon reinforced my brooding mood.

For the first time in my life, I understood that God accepted me whatever my disposition – happy or sad, loving or angry. God was neither capricious nor arrogant (as I had sometimes thought him to be), but was consistently supportive and generously loving. I did not elect to be his child – he elected to be my Father.

Too, I developed something of a world view. I had never been out of the Southeast before. Now I was all the way across the continent in an "other-world" sort of place – and God was here, too. I felt his presence just as the psalmist found God wherever he went.

Sometimes Mildred, whom I had come to appreciate more and more, joined me on the roof, but she had a short interest span and found little satisfaction in the quietude. "For me to worship," she said, "I need lots of singin' and preachin' and amen-shoutin'."

I found myself directing prayers toward Mildred's welfare. I had come to see her as a product of her deprived childhood, just as I was a product of mine. She wasn't "shiftless" or "low-down" because she was black, as some of the people back home would have said. Yet, in a way, she was what she was because she was black. Her being born black had done to her what my being born to a sharecropper had done to me. We had worked out our problems in different ways, and I loathed her way, yet I couldn't condemn her for it. I could imagine how tempting it must have been for her, at age fifteen, to accept her first money from a man.

For the first time, I was praying for someone in an unselfish way. True, I had prayed for my father and my family, and especially Papa Leslie, but I had a vested interest in these persons. With Mildred, it was different. My heart went out to her solely because she was a fellow human being in need. I wanted something better for her, and I felt that if there was to be a change, God would have a hand in it.

Somehow, focusing on Mildred helped me to tolerate my own lot. For the first time in my life, I recognized there were people who had come up harder than I had. I had experienced the harsh side of life, but not the seamy side. This close-up acquaintance would, in future times, help me to relate to all sorts of people and enable me to portray characters that otherwise I would not have understood.

This isn't to say that I wasn't impatient to get out to Hollywood. I was more eager than ever now. I felt that God was going to send me to Hollywood as soon as he was through using me at 116 South Hope Street.

I know that time has a way of prettying up our memories, but when I look back on my days in detention, I sense that God was with me, using my days of confinement to bring me to a higher level of freedom than I had known before.

I had been in the center three weeks when I received a letter from my mother. She had been terribly worried about me and was writing on the outside chance that the center would know my new address and forward it. The day she received my letter, she sat down and wrote the center, asking that I be permitted to go my way. She presumed this had happened, although she had not heard from either the officials or me.

On several occasions, I had asked Mother Baskin when I would be released. Each time, she insisted that she was waiting until she received a letter from my parents saying I wasn't a fugitive or a runaway and had means for financial support.

Upon receiving my mother's letter, I went to the housemother's room and confronted her with it. She said she had not received the earlier letter that my mother mentioned.

"But I can promise you that your case will be handled expeditiously," she said. "I'll see to it."

The next morning, about ten o'clock, a police wagon rolled up. We were curious to see who was going to take a ride. I was surprised when they called from downstairs, "Mickey Sauls, please report to the desk." Maybe they were going to release me and give me a ride into town!

"Well, Mickey," Mother Baskin said, "at last you're getting to go home. I'm so glad for you."

"But I don't want to go home!" I protested. "Don't you understand? I want to go to Hollywood!"

"Mickey!" the housemother said. "You'll be much better off at home with your family."

"I'm sorry, miss," one of the two policemen broke in, "but we have a court order to put you on the 10:30 train to Chicago. From there you will go to Atlanta, and then on home."

Since childhood, I had spent my life trying to get to Hollywood, and now that I was on its doorstep, they were robbing me of the opportunity — maybe the last one I'd get.

I became hysterical. I got down on my knees and begged. I told them about the hardships I had faced, and about my urgent ambitions.

"There's nothing that you can say or do that will change things," one of the policemen said. "You're a vagrant, and the city and county aren't willing to accept responsibility for you. Get yourself and your things together, and let's go. It's getting late."

The policemen pulled me, kicking and screaming, out of the center and into their car. On Mother Baskin's orders, Mildred got my things into my suitcase. As she put it into the car, she gave me a hug and whispered in my ear, "Cheer up. Things will work out. God loves you. Remember telling me that?"

The conductor was already boarding passengers when we walked up. One of the policemen handed me my suitcase while the other pressed my ticket into my hand.

The conductor took my bag and swung it up onto the boarding platform of the coach, then reached for my ticket.

"I don't want to get on this train," I said. "Mister, let me tell you my side of the story, please."

"We're pulling out, ma'am," he said. "Please climb aboard."

I backed up and was ready to run when the policemen caught me on either arm and lifted me onto the platform. There was a blast of the whistle; the conductor waved a signal to the engineer, and the train pulled out.

"Aren't you even going to listen to me?" I demanded of the conductor.

"Listen, lady, there's not one thing that I can do," he said, walking away. He came back and added, "We're going to be taking a long ride together – all the way to Kansas City, where I get off. I advise you not to try to leave this train. If you jump off while we're running, you'll get hurt; and if you try to slip off during a stop, we'll have the police onto you in no time."

I plopped into the first empty seat and kept my face to the

window for the longest time. I was humiliated. I had been manhandled. I was riding on a ticket marked "charity," which galled me when I remembered how my family had proudly refused government assistance through the years. Apparently I was still a prisoner. And everybody in the coach had gawked at me. Likely they were still staring.

I went to the rest room and washed my face, combed my hair, and applied new make-up. Back at my seat, I slipped on my jacket. At the very next stop, I would get off. I dared not try to take my suitcase with me — I would forget about it.

When we stopped, I checked and saw the conductor in the next car. I went to the vestibule and waited until I heard the signal for the train to pull out. Then I jumped.

The conductor saw me just as he swung back onto the train. "Hey!" he shouted. "Stop that girl!"

I ran. Smack into the biggest policeman I've ever seen. Back on the train I went.

"Listen," the conductor said. "You might as well understand that you aren't going to get off this train. Police in every town in California that we pass through have been alerted to be on the lookout for you, and when we cross over into Nevada, I'll personally see that you don't get off."

During the long ride, I frequently got into arguments with myself. One part of me said, "That was an absurd idea you had, striking out for Hollywood with no money to live on. Why did you think you could get a job in movies — haven't thousands as talented as you failed? You're better off headed home, where people know you and where you aren't going to starve."

The other part of me said: "If you weren't destined to go to Hollywood, you wouldn't feel the urge so deeply. You could be a success yet, if they'd only let you. You've got to get off this train."

With this voice in command, I considered my alternatives. If I got off in the desert, I would perish. If I got off in a town, I would be captured — unless. Unless they didn't recognize me! My best chance would be in Kansas City, where the conductor would go off duty. If I had extra luck, he would forget to caution the new conductor about me.

We arrived in a drizzle. The passengers for Kansas City left the train, and I saw the conductor get his satchel and step off. He was stopped by a big, red-faced man in a ten-gallon hat and black boots. Somebody wanting to know which train this is, I said to myself.

When the conductor had gone, I opened my suitcase and got out my raincoat, a floppy rain hat, and a scarf. I pulled the hat brim down, covering most of my face, and I wrapped the scarf so that it came up on my chin. I stepped off the train and walked briskly toward the steps to the terminal waiting room. I heard footsteps behind me and a moment later felt a hand grasp my arm. Two black boots were walking beside me. Then the hand pulled me around and said, "Where do you think you're going, sis?"

I looked up and saw the red face and the ten-gallon hat.

"I'm a railroad detective," he said. "The conductor warned me you'd probably try to get off here."

I broke and ran.

"Stop her!" the detective yelled.

A redcap let the handle of his luggage carrier fall. He stood in front of me with his legs and arms outstretched the way we used to corner chickens in the garden. "Pardon me, miss," he said, "but Mr. John says I gotta kotch you." Which he did.

When the detective came up, I kicked his shin as hard as I could. As he was jumping up and down and cursing, there was a flash of light. A man with a large camera had captured the detective doing his dance while the redcap struggled to hold me.

"What is she charged with?" the photographer asked.

"Oh, she isn't charged with anything," the detective said. "She went out to Hollywood to become a movie star, but she didn't have a penny to her name, so the authorities put her on this train to send her home." He rubbed his leg. "Take it from me," he said, "she's a hellcat!"

With that, he limped back to the train, pulling me along, and searched out the conductor. "This is the one who gave Eustice all the trouble," he said. "She'll bear extra watching."

"Thanks, Sam, I'll keep my eye on her."

When we pulled out of Kansas City, I realized I'd just as well accept my situation. What good would it do me to escape? Without money, I couldn't buy a bus ticket, and I wasn't desperate enough to try hitchhiking. So I took a seat and resigned myself to continuing the journey.

At St. Louis, a reporter and a photographer came aboard to take a picture and interview me. The Kansas City newsman's story and photo had been distributed by a press association.

"They say you're a hellcat," the reporter said. "Why do they say that?"

Resentment churned up inside me, but realizing that I had a national audience if I wanted it, I related my side of the story: how I had worked hard in the fields, struggled to get an education, and, just when an opportunity to pursue my chosen career appeared, my rights as an American citizen had been violated. Hopeful that some producer might see the write-up, I included details about the beauty pageants and theatrical director job.

When the press associations spread my picture from coast to coast, newsmen started coming aboard at every major stop, and at some small towns, as well. Soon passengers coming aboard recognized me.

In Evansville, Indiana, a man and his wife and little daughter boarded. The child cried, "It's her! It's her!"

"It's who?" her mother asked.

"The lady whose picture was in the paper. The one they called a — you know — that bad word."

"She means 'hellcat,' " her father said.

"Robert, I asked you not to use that word around Cynthia. And Cynthia, don't point and don't talk so loud."

Several times during the next hour, the girl tugged at her mother and asked permission to come over and talk to me, but each time she was refused.

"I really don't mind, ma'am," I said to the mother.

She reacted as though I had contaminated them. "Cynthia, you get in your seat and stay there," she ordered, giving me another dirty look.

Much later, the father went back to the smoking car and the mother went to the rest room. Cynthia edged over to me.

"Are you really a hellcat — whatever that means?"

"No, dear, maybe a *hurt* cat, but not a hellcat."

"You don't seem to have any friends."

"It looks that way, doesn't it?"

"But I want to be your friend," she said.

"Thank you. And I'd like to be your friend, too," I said, patting her soft, blond curls.

When the mother returned, she snatched the girl away from me and yanked her back into her own seat.

"But Mother, she isn't really a hellcat. She just doesn't have any friends. I want to be her friend."

The mother slapped the child and glowered at her for several minutes. I wanted to intervene but didn't dare.

I was touched. The child had reached out to me although she knew it would displease her mother. She was brave, honest, and generous. And when she said I had no friends, she came close to the truth. Certainly, I had no friend except her on that train. And outside my family and Ollie, I didn't have many friends, period. The thought made me sad.

But I knew I had another friend, who had been with me on my journey to Hollywood and back. That friend was God. There had been many disappointments that I couldn't understand, and I wanted to cry out to God, "Why, why, why?" But I also recognized that I would have been crushed had God not been with me.

I had acted foolishly. God knew I had. He was trying now to tell me just how foolish I had been. Still, I wanted to charge my escapade off to my youth and inexperience. I felt that God heard this excuse, too.

I made a solemn promise to myself to return to Hollywood. God would give me another opportunity. I would be ready.

12

"let's get married right now!"

The Los Angeles County Welfare Department had wired my parents when to expect me, and Daddy and Ollie were at the station. I gave each of them a hug and a kiss. The embraces felt good, yet I found myself pulling back as a child pulls back when reunited with a parent from whom he has been separated. Although I was the one who had run off, I was so full of hurt and bewilderment that I wanted to cry out, "Where were you two when I needed you?" I *felt* like a child — an errant child — and I feared that Ollie and Daddy saw me that way, just as the authorities had.

There was another reason for me to pull away from Ollie. I felt dirty, and I *was* dirty. I was grimy from the long, sooty, and sometimes steamy train ride. But I also felt "soiled" by the events of the last several weeks.

I answered Ollie's and Daddy's questions tersely. I wanted to let my wounds heal, not reopen them. At home, following more hugs and kisses and some tears, I faced a barrage of questions. Finally, I said I didn't feel well and wanted to go to bed. I wanted to go to sleep and block out all thoughts of the cross-country debacle. I wanted to wake up and find it had been a bad dream.

There was a problem I had not anticipated. Continued notoriety. Each day brought armloads of letters and cards. There were offers of help, some accompanied by cash or checks. I returned the money — if I hadn't done so on my own, Daddy would have required it. There were notes of sympathy, expressions of indignation against the authorities, and proposals of marriage. There were also nasty letters saying that if my parents had raised me right, I wouldn't have become a prodigal daughter.

At first, I relished the attention, but I soon had a surfeit. It became a physical and financial impossibility for me to answer even the most appealing communications, so I started screening out cash and checks and burning the correspondence unread. I hoped my hurt and humiliation would go up in the smoke.

Once again, I did a man's work in the fields. Anyone who put his feet under my father's table worked, and although I had the usual disdain of a young woman of nineteen for sweaty labor and the usual fondness of soft hands, I never for a moment questioned returning to the role of field hand. I was terribly afraid I would provoke my father to say, "So you think you're too good now?"

Actually, working in the fields provided me with a catharsis. The good earth, with its fresh air and honest soil, connected me with God, the creator. I could celebrate his being master of the heavens and earth, birds of the air and beasts of the field — and *my* master, too, since I was part of this same world. I didn't let myself dwell on another of God's creatures, man. I had seen so much that was cruel and sordid, I wondered if I would ever be open and trusting again.

Since my drudgery required my body but not my mind, I pondered the direction that my future should take once I became strong enough to assault life once more. Only my *near* future was at issue; as to my ultimate future, there was no question. I was going back to Hollywood, and next time I would make it. I would be wiser, better prepared. My motivation to succeed was stronger than before, for I had added a great many people to my "I'll just show you!" list.

At the same time, my recent experience put me on the defensive with God. I could not help but wonder if he had sent me to California to test me, as he had dispatched Bible characters to strange lands. I concluded that the fiasco "just happened" owing to a conspiracy of human failures, some of them my own. God still intended for Hollywood to be the arena for my becoming somebody, but he expected me to make a larger contribution to this effort.

After a few weeks on the farm, I recognized that I had to quit humoring myself. I had gotten myself into that jam in Los Angeles. Also, as I looked behind my jaundiced view of humanity, I saw that many persons had been remarkably generous with me. Mildred, for example, and the house-mother. Even the molls, who had been so menacing, had contributed to my personal growth. The theatrical company which I had left in a lurch had been forgiving. And Ollie and my family had been kinder than I had any right to expect.

My ambition and harsh childhood had led me to believe that I was *owed* success in films, but Aunt Mary had been closer to the truth when she said that opportunity wasn't going to come hunting for me − I would have to flush out opportunity, chase it down, seize it. So, with the twin goals of earning money and learning to deal with people again, I took a secretarial job with an insurance agency in Macon.

I rented a room in a boarding house, but most weekends I returned to Henry Springs. The reason: Ollie. Since coming home from Los Angeles, I was seeing Ollie more and more. He had finished his course in Atlanta and was helping to look after his family's farming interests: We now had standing dates for Friday night and Sunday afternoon. Dear Ollie! He never blamed me for the Hollywood disaster − he only seemed bewildered by it all. He sensed my hurt and softened it − mostly by just being there.

One Sunday afternoon − December 11, 1938 − Ollie was taking me from Henry Springs to Davisville, where I would catch the six o'clock train to Macon. We were cruising along singing crazy songs like "Mairzy Doats," "The Hut Sut Song," and "The Three Little Fishes." Then, for no apparent reason, Ollie became very quiet.

"Let's get married!" he said.

"Married?" I feigned surprise. Actually, I had wondered when Ollie was going to ask. I had seen he was becoming serious, and I found myself liking him more and more, too. But, in a way, I had dreaded his proposing. I didn't know what my answer should be. On the one hand, I wanted Ollie – certainly I didn't want to lose him forever by saying no. On the other hand, I couldn't shut myself off from a screen career by saying yes. I had to continue working, save money, become and remain independent.

"Married?" I repeated, trying to turn his sudden proposal into a joke. "Why, Ollie, I can't marry you. You don't love me enough to marry me."

"The heck I don't," he said. He reached over and pulled me toward him. I slid over against him. "If I didn't love you," he said, "would I be sitting here proposing? No, I mean it. Let's get married – right now!"

"Oh, Ollie, I've got a job in Macon, remember? You've got to get me to the train. This is no time for us to get married."

"You aren't answering me, Mickey."

I didn't want to answer; I wanted to wipe the question off the slate. If I stalled, would Ollie drop me? He might, for he was the proud type who might take delay for rejection. But if I didn't marry Ollie, how long would I have to work at my present job, or some other job that I detested? Was I going to let my Hollywood fantasy kill my dream of someday getting married and having children and a nice home of my own? If I said no now, would it get easier and easier for me to say no? What would my parents say about me marrying Ollie? True, I was a grown woman for all practical purposes – still, I was only twenty years old. I was forever coming back to live with my folks, so maybe I at least owed them the courtesy of discussing Ollie's proposal with them.

As these questions and others ran through my mind, I heard Ollie insisting, "Tell me now, Mickey. Tell me now!"

"Oh, Ollie, I don't know. . . ."

"Let's do it, right now!"

"But Ollie, it's Sunday. We'd have to find a preacher. Besides, we don't even have a license."

"Mickey — I dare you!" In my mind's ear, I heard him saying, "Mickey — I *love* you!" Ollie was looking straight into my eyes, and I felt he was reading my mind and knew my great desire to yield.

"Well, why not?" I exclaimed. "Okay, we'll just get married!"

Ollie pulled my chin up and kissed me. The car ran onto the shoulder, and instead of guiding it back, he pulled off the road and stopped. As we held each other and shared a long kiss, I became aware that Ollie was looking at his watch. "Gosh, it's late," he said, breaking away. "We'd better get going."

"To the train?"

"No, to find a justice of the peace!"

Ollie drove to the courthouse. The building was locked. But just as he walked back to the car, we saw Judge Gregory of the ordinary's court coming out a side door.

"Hey, Judge Gregory!" Ollie shouted. "We want to get married!"

The judge squinted at Ollie. "You're the Jordan boy, aren't you? And who's the lucky lady?"

"That's Miss Sauls — Mickey Sauls from out at Henry Springs."

"And you want to get married?"

"Yessir, and we're in sort of a hurry!"

"Is that so?"

"Yessir. You see, she's got to catch a train."

"A train? Well, the more questions I ask, the more confused I get. You both of age?"

"Yessir. Could you do it right now?"

"I reckon so," he said, smiling. "Y'all come on in."

"If you don't mind, Judge Gregory, could we wait for you out here? As I said, we're kinda in a hurry."

The judge looked nonplussed; nevertheless, he went into the courthouse and got the necessary papers. He slid into the front seat beside me, filled out the papers, and affixed his seal. The judge read the vows, Ollie and I said "I do," and he wound it all up with something about the authority vested in him and "I pronounce you husband and wife." He gave Ollie the license; Ollie handed him five dollars. He wished us well, got into his own car, and drove off.

Ollie and I sat looking at each other; then, with a laugh, we threw ourselves into each other's arms.

"We're married!" Ollie shouted.

It had happened so quickly. "Ollie, are we really married? I mean, I've heard that transactions on Sunday aren't legal — and besides, we didn't have any witnesses."

"You just try to get out of it!" Ollie said. He glanced at his watch. "Why, it's a quarter to six. We'd better skedaddle."

I didn't want to catch that train. I wanted to call the company and tell them I had quit — or was sick. I wanted to relish, for a few hours at least, being "Mrs. O. H. Jordan, Jr." But I didn't say anything. Maybe it *was* better for me to go to Macon. It would give me time to sort out my thoughts. We'd been married only twenty minutes and already I was wondering if I'd made a mistake.

"If you have to," Ollie said, "give the company two weeks' notice, but see if they won't agree to one week. I'll come up and get you. I need to keep our marriage secret for a little while — until I can get things worked out. Could you stay with your folks?

"Ollie! You're kidding!"

"No, I've never been more serious in my life."

The train was already in when we pulled up and parked. I went and bought my ticket while Ollie asked the conductor to wait for me. A hurried kiss, an awkward exchange of "Goodby, Mickey," "Goodby, Ollie," and I was gone.

As the train clacked its way northward, its mournful whistle piercing the silent, darkening countryside, I felt empty. What a shallow way to begin a marriage! Years from now, what would we have to remember? When we were in the company of other people and they recalled their wedding nights, would we remain silent, or would we dare relate that Ollie had gone home to his folks and I had taken a train to Macon? Our marriage seemed cheap. I couldn't even tell anyone I was married. Was Ollie ashamed of me? Why had I married him? Was it because I really loved Ollie — loved him enough to spend the rest of my life with him? Or, was it because marrying him made me somebody? He was well-bred, came from an affluent family, was good-looking, had a car and spending money, would likely take over the family farming interests. Had I married Ollie for Ollie, or for the opportunity to gain things missing from my own life? Could I give myself completely to him, or to anyone, for that matter?

What would my marriage do to my plans to become a movie star? I would be giving up my job, my only chance to save money. Maybe unbeknownst to Ollie, I could put a little bit away every chance I got. But that would take years! A thousand times, I had told Ollie how much Hollywood meant to me, but he never seemed to take me seriously.

If I asked his permission, well, he'd most likely say no. And what would I do then?

You're reaching too far, Mickey. Right now, you'll do well just to get used to the idea of being married. You've got to start thinking of Ollie instead of just yourself. Learn to love him "in sickness and in health." If you learn to love him, and if he really loves you, he'll gladly let you go to Hollywood.

It sounded good, but would it ever happen? I doubted that O. H. Jordan, Jr., would ever permit his wife to go to Hollywood to seek her fortune.

Fat chance!

Two weeks after our curbside ceremony, my new husband drove to Macon to get me. I was sitting on the lawn in front of my boarding house.

Ollie didn't even kiss me. He went inside and got my suitcase and some boxes and threw them in the back, then wrestled my locker into the trunk. I waited for him to come around and open my door for me. I guess that if I hadn't gotten in by myself, I'd still be in front of the boarding house. He had the car rolling before I was in good.

I've made a terrible mistake, I thought to myself. For two weeks, I had questioned whether our jumped-up marriage could succeed, and apparently Ollie had been having the same thoughts. How can two strangers be marriage partners? I wondered.

This isn't the man I want to spend the rest of my life with! I want someone warm. I want someone who will be proud to have me as his wife, not keep our marriage secret.

We drove several miles and finally Ollie asked, "How've you been?"

"Fine, and you?"

"I've been okay, too." There was silence again. Then we swapped more trivia. I wanted to jump out of the car and run.

Ollie delivered me to my parents' house, lugged my things in, and departed. Maybe he figured that with my acting experience I could live a lie better than he could.

Ollie came over almost every night, which broke the terrible monotony and softened my resentment of the drudgery, but I hated saying goodby. If we were married, we ought to live married. The middle of the week, Ollie came and gave me a diamond and a wedding band, making our marriage seem more official — even so, I couldn't wear them.

"Give me a few more days," he pleaded. "I'll get things worked out." But the few more days brought no new developments.

On Saturday, one week after my homecoming, Ollie and I were sitting in his car in our yard when my father came out and confronted us with the rings. Bobbie, it seems, had been nosing around in my pocketbook and found them. Naturally, she couldn't resist sharing her great discovery.

"Well," Daddy demanded, "are you married?"

"We — we're just thinking about it," I said.

"Are you sure?"

"Yessir."

Without saying another word, Daddy got into his old car

and took off. I suspected what he was up to, and when Ollie said he had to go, I said, "Nosiree, you aren't leaving me to wiggle out of this alone."

A short while later, Daddy came back.

"You're lying," he said. "You're married and the courthouse records show it."

With our eyes, we acknowledged the truth of his accusation.

"No daughter of mine's gonna be party to a secret marriage," Daddy said. "You're married and you're gonna live together out in the open."

"But Daddy — "

"There ain't no 'but' to it," he said, stalking off.

The next afternoon, Ollie moved me to his house. When we arrived, his family was assembled in the living room waiting for us. I had caught my skirt in the front door, and entering the room with a ripped-out hem made me feel more edgy and embarrassed. After I had moved around the circle exchanging how-do-you-do's, Ollie's Aunt Daisy suggested that she mend my skirt. She led me down the hall to the bathroom and closed the door. I sensed that she aimed to mend something other than my dress.

"I know it isn't easy to come into a new family," she said. "It makes you feel — well, so on display. We don't mean to hang back. We know we're going to love you, and you love us. But maybe you can understand the situation better if you know how we've always doted on O. H. Junior. When he came in and told us you had married secretly — well, it came as a great shock. Naturally, his daddy and mother aren't overjoyed right now."

"I understand."

"But I know you're the right one for him. If you weren't then the good Lord wouldn't have brought the two of you together." She tied the thread and bit off the loose ends. "Now, let's go and give the rest of them a chance to get to know you."

I could understand why Ollie had acted so strangely when

he picked me up in Macon. He was experiencing the same misgivings that I was, and the fear that news of our marriage would leak out frightened him. He knew that he would eventually have to tell his family, and he dreaded the prospect.

As the evening progressed, I began to feel better. Clearly, the Jordans were going to do their best to accept me, and it relieved me to know that a compassionate and gracious Aunt Daisy was going to help me understand and accept them. But best of all, after supper Ollie led me out onto the porch. He took me in his arms and kissed me. "I'm glad it's out in the open," he said. "I hated leaving you every night."

"I wanted you to stay terribly," I sighed.

We rejoined his family and, after a polite span of time, said goodnight. Ollie led me to his bedroom, which his mother had thoughtfully redecorated, adding a touch of feminity here and there.

"I'm glad we got married," Ollie said.

"So am I."

"Those two weeks that you were in Macon seemed like a long, long time."

"I know."

During the night, a small tree limb fell on the roof directly over our bedroom. It woke me, but Ollie slept on. I snuggled up to him, and it felt good having someone to be close to. Maybe our marriage was going to work, after all.

As the weeks rolled by, a variety of circumstances conspired to drive a wedge between us. For one thing, we were living in the house with Ollie's family. At times, I felt as though I were intruding upon them; at other times, I felt invaded. I desperately wanted to get Ollie off to myself.

Also, I got bored. Not only was there no field work for me, but also, because there was a cook and maid, there was no housekeeping except to tidy up our bedroom. I read novels and movie magazines, along with some books on acting and direction. Ollie, on the other hand, stayed terribly busy — so busy that I grew jealous of his work and felt guilty over my idleness.

Ollie sensed that I was growing restless, and he bought me a beautiful horse which I named Prissy Pal. Afternoons, I made lemonade and rode out to wherever Ollie happened to be working and spent a few minutes with him. These brief periods spent alone with him were delightful.

One morning, six weeks after we were married, I woke up and smelled ham cooking. I instantly became deathly sick. I skipped breakfast and stayed in our room the rest of the day.

I continued to be nauseated and began living on ice, lettuce, and soda crackers. Late one morning, I went to the kitchen for some black coffee and a piece of dry toast.

"I'm beginning to get suspicious," my mother-in-law said.

"Suspicious? Of what?"

"That you may be pregnant."

"Me? Pregnant? Surely not. I mean, I hadn't even thought of the possibility. Do you think that may be my trouble?"

"Well, morning sickness is a common sign of pregnancy," interjected Marjorie, Ollie's sister.

My mother had suffered nausea with each of us, but I hadn't related her experiences to my own situation. Having babies was for other people, not for me. Oh, I wanted to have a family — sometime — but certainly not before I had established myself in a movie career.

"Mickey," Mrs. Jordan said, "I think we'd better make an appointment with the doctor. He might be able to give you something to relieve your nausea."

I saw the doctor that afternoon. He thought I was pregnant but couldn't confirm it. He gave me some medicine, along with advice on what to eat and drink. Nothing helped. I grew sicker and sicker, until I was spending practically all day in bed and in the bathroom. Sometimes I was so weak I couldn't hold my head up. I didn't care whether I lived or died.

When my pregnancy was confirmed, I began to regard it as a loathsome disease that would leave me handicapped. I would be tied down and I would never get to Hollywood!

Ollie had done this to me, and I told him so. Dear easy-going Ollie had been so concerned, so compassionate – and so sympathetic that some mornings he himself couldn't eat breakfast. Ollie was slow to anger, but when he blew, he blew! I continued to berate him, and one day he gave me a piece of his mind:

"There are two of us in this, remember? Don't blame me as though you had nothing to do with it. Also, you're acting awfully selfish. Here God's about to bless us with a baby and all you think about is what's going to happen to your movie career – which at this point is still just a dream in your head. I'm sorry you're so sick, but don't make yourself even more miserable by bemoaning what's happened. This baby can be a joy if you'll only let it."

"You're a fine one to talk," I cried. "You don't have to be sick, or carry the baby, or go through labor, or nurse it all day long. It isn't going to interfere with your career one bit. Naturally you aren't upset. Why should you be?"

Ollie stalked out, and in the weeks that followed, I grew quieter and Ollie became withdrawn.

Then, one beautiful spring morning, it happened. I felt life stirring within me. In that moment, I accepted my child as a gift from God. The sensation of butterfly wings brushing inside me was God's way of telling me to get ready for this wondrous manifestation of his love. No longer was my baby an "it," but a person – a "he" or a "she." I wondered which it would be. I thought Ollie wanted a son, so I hoped it would be a boy. Still, I couldn't help but think how much fun it would be to have a daughter.

Oh, dear God, I've been so wicked – first rejecting the love you brought to me in the person of Ollie, and then resenting this new life you're giving us. I feel so ashamed, not wanting my own child. Forgive me, Lord. I'll be a good wife and mother yet. I'll try awfully hard, really I will!

From that moment, I cherished my opportunity of becoming a mother. My nausea gradually disappeared.

Gayle was beautiful – blonde and blue-eyed like her father.

She was tiny and delicate, weighing only four pounds. Her complete dependence upon me made me feel important and needed, and looking after her filled the voids in my days. She was a bond between Ollie and me.

Gayle was only six months old when I started getting nauseated again. This time, I knew I was pregnant. I wasn't prepared for this, but I remembered how upset I had been the first time – and how wrong I had been. So, this time I tried to accept my situation.

When Sandra arrived, she was like me, with huge, black eyes and a head full of black hair. Now I had two babies to love – and two babies to care for. I had few idle moments, no time to waste in reflection or daydreaming. My dominant feeling was fulfillment as a woman.

I should have anticipated that my roller-coaster life would toboggan again. For one thing, I didn't feel good. Ill health plagued me following Sandra's birth. A series of miscarriages and surgical procedures left me unable to have more children. I had wanted so very much to give Ollie a son.

But the most ravaging disease I suffered was that gnawing Hollywood dream. With Sandy toddling about getting into everything and Gayle still needing almost constant attention, I began doubting if I would ever get a crack at that movie career. Then, almost overnight it seemed, I found myself celebrating my twenty-fifth birthday. My self-image began deteriorating. I no longer pictured myself as young, gay, attractive, entertaining. I felt old – and trapped.

Ollie knew what he wanted out of life, and he seemed to be getting it. My problem was, he seemed to know what he wanted *me* to get out of life, too – exactly what I was getting. It wasn't enough.

I tried to talk to Ollie and he tried to listen, but he couldn't possibly hear me. My lifelong vision of going to Hollywood was as impossible for him to comprehend as it would have been for me to propose that we vacation in Antarctica. When I tried to share my burning ambitions with him, he would say, "But Mickey, *this* is where you belong. Gayle, Sandy, and I love you, and we need you! I just can't believe you're serious about wanting to go off and leave us. Why don't we plan a picnic next Sunday afternoon? Getting out in the open will do you good."

Eventually, I recognized that Ollie would never understand my dream. He didn't feel what I felt. He'd never been a nobody striving desperately to become a somebody. I would just have to go. I would face the consequences, whatever they might be, when I got back.

It was almost as though Ollie had been reading my mind. Just as I was about to put my desperate plan into action, he sought to relieve my unhappiness by taking me out of the house with my in-laws. He moved us to Glendale, a quiet little town of schools and churches, twenty miles from Davisville. There he opened a farm implement business.

Lunchtime and evenings, Ollie came home full of his business and its future — full of this new community and its good people and the good life that it offered.

I detested Ollie's blueprint for our lives, but I had stopped opposing it verbally:

"Yes, it is a very nice town."

"Yes, it's a wonderful place to rear our daughters."

"Yes, I'm sure I'll learn to like the people once the children are a bit older and I can get out and mix more."

I said "yes," but inside I screamed "no!" More distressing, I knew that I would continue to say "no" to life as long as I was fenced off from my Hollywood dream.

I was going! Ollie would just have to accept it. He had simply come along too late. At the time I married him, I was already married — to a dream.

And when he went off to the Army, I consummated that earlier marriage.

hollywood: land of illusion

"This is *my* day! It's here!"

I would meet with Barney Dean at nine, and later I would lunch with Bob Hope, who was to arrange a screen test for me. Except for my ordeal with the drunk bellhop, which now seemed nothing more than a bad dream, things had worked out fine. I was confident that this trip to Hollywood — unlike my first — would be a big success.

I had been awakened by chimes from the church across the street. I indulged in a luxurious stretch as I went to the window. The church was as beautiful by day as at night. Below my window, people were scurrying along the sidewalks on their way to work. Already, traffic was heavy.

I was about to step into the shower when someone knocked on my door.

"Yes?"

A female voice said, "The manager thought you might like coffee and the morning paper."

I wrapped myself in a bath towel and opened the door. "I sure could use a cup of coffee," I said. I faced a pretty brunette with the classic face of a model — high cheekbones and all — and a gorgeous smile. She came in, set her tray down, and poured my coffee.

131

"Cream and sugar?" she asked.

"No, black, please. I'm in a bit of a hurry. I have a nine o'clock appointment at Paramount."

"Oh, Paramount. Well, don't let me detain you."

"I'm to see Bob Hope."

"He's nice. Have you met him already?"

"No, but I met his associate, Barney Dean."

"He's nice, too. You'll like him."

"Do you know Barney?"

"Not very well."

"You seem to be well acquainted with Paramount," I said, sipping the steaming coffee. "How far is it out there?"

"It's only ten minutes by taxi."

"Good, then I have time to drink my coffee. I'm riding over in the courtesy car. Won't you have some coffee, too? Is there another cup handy?"

"No, thank you. I really don't want any."

"My name is Mickey Jordan. What's yours?"

"Olga Svetnik — I mean Barnett. It's hard for me to get used to my married name."

"Glad to meet you, Olga. Tell me, what should I wear? I thought I'd wear a fitted suit. This one. Do you think it would be right?"

"I like it. Do you have a bright blouse?"

"Yes. Does this look okay?"

"Great!"

Olga brought an ironing board and insisted upon pressing my blouse while I showered. As I dressed, I picked out of her how I should conduct myself, what I should say and not say.

"I've got to get back to the coffee shop now," she said. "I'll be dying to hear how things went. Stop by and let me know."

I fixed my hair and went downstairs. As I passed through the lobby, I glimpsed Olga in the coffee shop, and we waved to each other.

A few minutes after the courtesy car delivered me to the

Paramount gate, Barney appeared.

"Mickey!" he said. "So you finally made it. It's good to see you again."

"Oh, Barney, I'm so happy, I think I'm going to cry. In fact, I *am* crying."

"Hey, I understand," he said, putting an arm around my shoulders. "It makes me happy to see you happy." He gave me his handkerchief and I dabbed at my eyes.

"Now that you're all repaired," Barney said, "let's go get breakfast. But if you aren't too hungry, I'd like us to take the scenic route."

"I'd love it. I'm really not hungry at all."

"Anything in particular you want to see?"

"Well, I suppose the cowboy set would be my first choice."

As we moved through "Dodge City," I was transported back in time to the Saturday afternoons of my childhood. I could see the guys in the black hats, their guns roaring, riding down the street past the saloon, jail, and hotel. Barney and I walked up to the newspaper office and he threw open the door. There was nothing behind it except a small patch of grass.

"So this is one of those false fronts I've read about," I said. "You'd never guess they were fakes."

"In Hollywood we have a lot of fake fronts that keep people guessing," Barney quipped, and we both laughed.

"I'm sorry there's no action on this set today," Barney said. "The crew's probably out at the ranch."

Barney bent over a boulder. Pretending to strain mightily, he lifted the big rock off the ground. Suddenly, he lifted it chest high and swung it around to me. "Here, you hold it a while," he said. It was papier-mache.

"Isn't anything real out here?" I laughed.

Barney stopped and picked up a nail. "Look at this," he said. The nail had two heads, one above the other. "This symbolizes Hollywood. The first head prevents the nail from going in too far, making it easy to pull out. One day there's a set, the next day it's gone. Nothing is permanent; few things run deep. At times the shallowness of it all kinda gets to you. But that's enough philosophizing for today."

"You're poetic, Barney. I'll keep the nail as a souvenir."

We viewed other sets — tenements, a railroad station, a ship at dockside, and others.

"Tell me about Bob Hope," I said.

"Oh, Leslie Townes Hope? Born in England — forty years ago, would you believe it? Came to this country with his family at age three; attended school in Cleveland, Ohio; went to work for the Chandler Motor Company — in retrospect, a most implausible job. But he didn't stay long. The stage beckoned. He toured for a while; formed his own company in Chicago; went on to New York and the RKO Vaudeville Circuit, then into radio and films. He's a great person, and a great humanitarian. We were proud when, back in January, the Poor Richard Club presented him their achievement award in recognition of his visits to our servicemen on the warfronts."

"Is he going back?"

"There are tentative plans for him to entertain troops in Europe this summer."

"How many 'Road' pictures has he made?"

"Four — Singapore, Zanzibar, Morocco, and Utopia. But I don't guess there's any end to them. Well, here's the commissary."

We ordered coffee and sweet rolls. Every time Barney started to take a bite, I'd ask him a question — mostly "Who's that over there?"

"Hey," Barney said, "I'm invited to a cocktail party tonight. The hostess always pulls together an interesting group. Maybe you'd like to come. I can wangle an invitation."

"Gee, I'd like to — that is, if I wouldn't be imposing." My tone let him know I wouldn't mind imposing just a little bit.

Barney went to a phone and called.

"It's all set," he said when he came back. "I'll pick you up at eight."

On our way to the sound stage where Bob was working on *Monsieur Beaucaire*, Barney told me about the picture. It was based on the Booth Tarkington novel. Rudolph Valentino had played the barber role in a film made in 1924. In the movie under production, Bob was forced to impersonate a notorious eighteenth-century French swordsman and ladykiller.

When we arrived, we confronted a red light flashing above a "No Admittance" sign. Barney walked me right past the guard. "We'll have to be absolutely still and absolutely quiet or they'll kick us out," he said as we went into the huge building.

We'd been watching ten minutes when the director called out, "Five-minute break."

Bob Hope, clad in a heavy coat trimmed with ermine and wearing a wig of long, powdered-white hair, walked offstage with several aides trailing. Barney waved and he came over.

"This is Mickey Jordan, Bob."

"Hi, Mickey. Welcome to the wonderful world of make-believe," he said, shaking hands. Meanwhile, a make-up man patted his perspiring face, another fellow picked lint off his jacket, and a third tried to get some unruly hair to lie down.

"Why don't we get some pictures, Barney?" Bob suggested.

Barney summoned a photographer, and Bob, Barney, and I struck a pose. As the photographer urged us to move closer together and to loosen up, I asked myself, "Can this be me posing with Bob Hope?" It was too good to be true.

When the filming resumed, Barney and I watched Bob try to discourage the king's daughter (Marjorie Reynolds), encourage a scullery maid (Joan Caulfield), and bluff a villainous general (Joseph Schildkraut). He was perfect for his part, hilarious whether at love or war.

At noon, Bob, Barney, and I had lunch at the commissary. Then, despite their protests that I would get tired, I spent the afternoon watching the filming. Barney joined me just before quitting time, and Bob invited us to his dressing room, which was a beautifully appointed trailer.

"Bob," Barney said, "I told Mickey you'd be glad to

arrange a screen test for her."

"Right," Bob said. He picked up the phone. "Get me Louis Shurr, please."

When his call was returned, Bob said, "Listen, pal, I've got a gorgeous Georgia peach here in my dressing room. . . . No, unfortunately old Barney boy is here with us, ha, ha. Friend, this girl is something. She can act, dance, and — what else do you do, Mickey? Sing — yes, she sings! Louis, I want you to make a star out of her. . . ."

He turned to me. "Can you meet Louis Shurr — he's an agent — at two tomorrow? He'll arrange the screen test. . . . Yep, that's okay, Louis. Thanks, pal."

I put out my hand. "Mr. Hope, how can I ever thank you?"

"It's my pleasure, Mickey. You've got the makings of a star, baby." He punctuated his statement with one of his famous tongue clicks.

As I rode back to the hotel in a cab, I was intensely happy. At long last, I had traded my cotton sack for a film career. But when I recalled how confidently the pros had worked before the cameras that day, I knew I had a long way to go. Still, I didn't have as far to go as I had already come.

It was after six when I got back to the hotel. Olga had gone home, leaving word that she would see me in the morning.

I got dressed and found I had twenty minutes before Barney would pick me up, so I decided to write Ollie a letter. After several starts, I gave up. No matter how elated I was, Ollie wasn't going to be able to share my happiness, because I had run out on him and our daughters. So, I wrote Mother instead. She would be thrilled.

At eight, Barney called me from the lobby and we drove to Hollywood. I was overwhelmed by the home of the hostess — a palace, really. It was constructed of pink marble. When Barney drove up to the portico, a uniformed servant greeted him by name, assisted me, then drove the car around back.

Some forty or fifty persons were already present when we walked into the exquisite drawing room. The hostess, a socialite rather than a professional in films, said she was so glad I was able to come to her "little" party. As Barney introduced me around, I recognized a dozen names and faces. These people were the stars, and I was impressed. However, I hadn't come to *be* impressed, but to *impress* — especially directors and producers.

"Barney, I'd like you to move around and have a good time. Just forget about me. I'm going to have to learn to get around for myself, and this will be a good place for me to see if I can."

The first seemingly important person I latched onto turned out to be a director. For the last three months, he had been cranking out flag-waving short features designed to sell war bonds, but he was about to direct a suspense thriller with half a dozen "biggies" in the cast.

"Oh, I'll bet that will be exciting," I said.

He allowed that it would not be exciting. The producer had already hired the cast, lined up the crew, approved the script, built the sets, decided what scenes would be shot and when, and assigned time and cost limits to each sequence. As director, he would merely do the nuts-and-bolts work, living up to the producer's specifications — or else. The producer and editor would decide which takes would be used and which wouldn't, he sighed, identifying the editor as "the wizard who makes sense out of nonsense" and the guy who determines the success of the project at the box office.

"But," I demurred, "you're the one who does the creative work."

Again not so, he said. "What's creative about covering up for a bum actor with an absurdly positioned camera or hiding an aging beauty's wrinkles with trick lighting?"

His sad story was more than I could bear. Besides, he wasn't interested in *my* story. So I moved on.

I joined a coterie gathered around a fat man in a white dinner jacket. I figured he was a top-rung executive. I soon learned that he was merely a hack writer, popular because of his repertoire of shady jokes.

The next target to come within my sights was a sure enough, bona fide producer. I said "hi," he said "hi," and the blonde with him said nothing. He got me a drink and asked me "Where have you been all my life?" or the equivalent, whereupon I began telling him. Three drinks later, we had gotten as far as my first trip to California, and he was still listening attentively. Then a fellow came up and broke the spell by asking how things were going.

He swirled his drink and looked into it, crystal-ball fashion. "Next year ought to be the best motion picture year ever," he said.

"Do you mean," I interrupted, "that we'll be seeing better pictures than ever before?"

"Hey, you do have a sense of humor," he said. "No – I mean the best year in terms of dollars, of course. The industry *ought* to take in two billion at the box office next year, mostly from films made this year."

"Two billion!" I repeated. "Wow!"

"I said it *ought* to be the best year. *But* –. There are a lot of buts. One is the fact that these damned unions are constantly striking or threatening to strike. Some strike because another union is striking, and sometimes the first union can't even remember what its grievance was. When you go to work in the morning, you never know who'll be there and who won't.

"And then there's the courts," he continued. "Paramount, for example, has tentatively been ordered to divest itself of its exhibition interests – its theaters. I'm for the independent producers – I'd like to see them succeed – but I think they're going to get nowhere and will, in the process, create chaos. These foreigners are going to come in and kill off both sides. And speaking of foreigners, this 'communist' business hasn't helped us, either."

I couldn't keep up with his drinking, and I didn't want to keep up with his dissertation. It was obvious we weren't going to get back to my story, so I sallied forth again.

The next group I looked in on was trying to quiet a pretty, but loud, young thing. She was cursing blue blazes because an older man — a noted actor and husband of a noted actress — had failed to show. "The lousy bum stood me up!" she wailed.

Barney joined me now and then to see how I was doing. "Just fine," I'd say, or "I'm having a ball." Actually, I was bored stiff and a bit unsure on my feet.

By midnight, many tongues had been loosened by a succession of alcohol baths. I recognized that I had had enough, so I took a seat in a corner. I observed one couple — married, but not to each other — sneaking upstairs.

The next time Barney checked on me, I said that although I hated to interrupt his evening, maybe I ought to get back to the hotel because I faced an important day. Barney, the perfect gentleman, drove me back to the hotel, thanked me for a nice evening, and predicted that I would "knock 'em cold" the next day.

I went into my room and sprawled across the bed. I felt sick, and I was furious at myself. Psychologically, I was exhausted and demoralized. I took a shower, got into bed, and slept soundly.

14

a letter from home

I was awakened by a knock on my door. I looked at my watch. It was nine-thirty.

"Mickey, it's me, Olga."

I jumped out of bed and opened the door. Olga held a tray. "I was afraid your breakfast was going to get cold before I could get you to open up," she said.

"Oh, Olga, you shouldn't have. You're spoiling me terribly."

Olga fluffed my pillows, motioned me into bed, and placed the tray in my lap.

"Now," she said, "tell me all about it."

My depression had vanished, and I excitedly told her about touring the Paramount lot with Barney, meeting Bob, and having an appointment with Louis Shurr that afternoon.

"Oh, I'm so happy for you," she said. "You're going to make it big!"

"I hope so. I've had this dream of becoming somebody for so very long. I've simply got to succeed — for the sake of my marriage, if for no other reason. If I fail, I don't believe I can go home and face Ollie."

"He's counting on you to do big things, huh?"

"No, he's counting on me to fail. That is, actually he isn't counting on anything. He doesn't even know where I am."

"Oh. And your little girls, who's looking after them?"

"My mother."

"Well, I'm sure that in a day or two you'll have big news for all of them."

"It'd better be in a day or two or I'll be flat broke."

"Tell me about the party you mentioned."

"Oh, Olga, I don't know. It was pretty horrible, really. I met some very nice people, but also some very unattractive and very boring people. So much of the conversation was put-on. And the way a few of those girls threw themselves at the directors and producers was sickening." I paused, invaded by feelings of regret. "Olga, the most frightening thing is that I was right in there trying to impress them, too."

"I know," Olga said. "Relationships can be so artificial. People can be so grasping. I didn't say anything about the fickle, seamy side of Hollywood yesterday because I didn't want to blunt your self-confidence, which, believe me, is essential. Oh, I don't mean to exaggerate. There are some great people out here – Bob Hope and Barney Dean, for example. But that's enough lecturing for today. I hope you'll pardon me for letting my hair down."

"Oh, I do. And I see what you're talking about, and it bothers me. I'm sure it bothers me more now than it would have when I was single. I'm not sure I can cope with the ruthless competition, the backbiting and all."

"Well, I suppose if you're good enough, you can be strictly professional and travel on your merits."

"But I haven't proved myself yet."

"You will. And this afternoon will be the start."

"Olga, there are some things you aren't telling me. I've got you pegged as having given up a pretty promising career in films."

"Oh, I don't know how promising it was, Mickey. At one time, I thought I was moving up pretty fast. My manager seemed to have a lot of confidence in me – and I certainly had confidence in him. He seemed so interested in me and my career. Then, one night, I learned it wasn't my *career* that he was interested in. It really shook me up. I guess it devastated my desire to work in films."

"So you got married?"

"Yes, I married the nicest guy you could ever meet. We'd been going together for three years. He worshiped me and pleaded with me to marry him, but I put him off because I didn't want to be tied down. I mean, I wanted to be tied down to Arthur, but I didn't want to jeopardize my career."

"And so you just walked out on it all?"

"Yes."

"And you've lived happily ever after?"

"I've been very happy," she said with a radiant smile. "I have no regrets."

"But – and I don't mean it in a derogatory way – you swapped a chance that most girls would give their eye teeth for to become – well, again, no offense, a waitress."

"A *good* waitress, I might add. And, I hope, a good wife."

"Boy, I don't know. . . ."

"I just had to find out who I was and what I wanted out of life. When I really explored that dream, which I had nurtured since childhood, I found it was empty. It would have collapsed years earlier if I hadn't kept puffing it up with air."

"I think I hear you telling me I ought to quit now."

"Oh, no, please. I wouldn't want you to misinterpret what I've said. I was talking strictly about *me*. If I've learned anything, I've learned that each person is different. No, a movie career may be your road to fulfillment. You'll do well, I'm sure. And you'll probably be happy at it too. So stop fretting."

"I feel terribly mixed up."

"Oh, Mickey, I'm so sorry I've done this to you. You need that same self-assurance you took with you yesterday. Eat your breakfast. I promise to be quiet."

"Olga, when that agent made the pass at you – or whatever it was that happened – did you just know right then that it was all over? How did you come to a final decision?"

"I prayed over it. I've always been a very religious person.

I tried to lay it all out before God, and he gave me the answer."

"Olga, could we pray right now?"

"Sure."

We bowed our heads. When I didn't say anything, Olga began:

"Dear Lord, be with Mickey as she wrestles with her hopes and fears. God, you and I both love her and we want her to find what's best for her. Direct her as she probes the innermost parts of her mind, heart, and soul. Help her to examine her life and your purposes for it fully and honestly. We ask this in Christ's name. Amen."

"Amen."

"Mickey, go out there this afternoon and give them your very best. Don't worry, if God doesn't intend for you to be a Hollywood star, he'll let you know. Now I've got to run."

"Well, I'm not so sure. For at least twelve years I've thought I heard him telling me one thing and now I'm wondering if he's telling me something else."

"I really must run, Mickey. Just remember, you've got a lot going for you. Call me when you get back. Here, I'll jot down my number."

I spent the next three hours getting ready for my afternoon appointment. When I was satisfied with my appearance, I went downstairs. I was going out the front door when the desk clerk called, "Mrs. Jordan, I'm so glad I caught you. A Paramount courier just brought this special delivery letter addressed to you in care of the studio. I rang your room and was afraid you were out."

The writing on the envelope was Mother's. I went up to my room, shut the door behind me, and leaned back against it. I dreaded opening the envelope. It was bad news – I just knew it was.

Mickey Darling,

Your babies are sick. They haven't eaten hardly at all since you left. All they do is cry, "I want my

Mommy, I want my Mommy." Ollie came home from Camp Wheeler on an overnight pass. I had to tell him you'd gone to California and left your girls with me. He was so upset and brokenhearted, he didn't eat a bite. All he did was to hold the babies close to him and cry. When it came time for him to go back to camp, he was the saddest person I've ever seen.

Mickey, please come home. Your babies and husband need you. I know you feel like you've got to do what you are doing. Maybe so, I don't know. But I just feel like now isn't the right time. If God intends for you to be a movie star, he'll let it happen at a time when it won't hurt other people so much. Do you really think he wants you to stay out there when your babies and your husband need you so bad? Who knows, Ollie may be shipped overseas anytime.

Mickey, if you could of looked in on us yesterday, you'd be on your way home right now. Please come home. Please!!!

We love you.   Mother

I stumbled to the bedside table and picked up the picture of Ollie and my babies. My eyes were so full of tears, I couldn't see them clearly. I sank to my knees. Outside, the church steeple was lighted with brilliant sunshine. My life had been filled with that kind of sunshine yesterday, but today it was cloudy and dark.

Dear God, help me. I know what you want me to do now, but dear Lord, I don't know how to do it. You're telling me to walk away from all this, but you know I don't want to. Still, I can't keep on living two lives; I know that.

I remember sitting on a cotton sack in a field on a hot night, hating my life and vowing to strike out and find a new one — a life that would provide me with the nice things other girls enjoyed. I wanted to be somebody — and not just for my own sake, but for my family, and for you, too, Lord. I

*wanted to succeed and then testify that I had faith in you
and you answered my prayers.*

*But now, just when success is so close I can taste it, you're
telling me to turn back. You're saying that becoming a
Hollywood actress isn't part of your plans for me. I know
that's so. If it wasn't, I wouldn't have gotten the letter in
time. Ten seconds and I'd have been out that door and on
my way.*

*But on my way to what? That's what you're asking me,
Lord. You're making me face up to reality. I've been telling
myself I could be a wife to Ollie and a mother to Gayle and
Sandra and be a Hollywood star at the same time, but I'd
never make it. I couldn't stand the pressure. My body
wouldn't bear up under the strain. My ambition would keep
gnawing at me. I'd never be satisfied, would I, Lord?*

*I can see all this, Lord, but I don't think I'm a strong
enough person to give it up. It's an obsession with me. It's in
my blood.*

*Lord, I can't − but I've got to! I'm ready to say yes to you
and no to my dream. I'd like to beg for one more chance −
just to go out there and take that screen test and prove to
myself and everybody else that I could have made it. But I
know you don't want that. If I walk out of this room and go
out to Hollywood, I'm walking out on you and my family,
and I can't do that. You know it wouldn't work anyhow.
So, I'm saying to you that I'm ready to accept your will
right now. But, Lord, you've got to help me. Cut this
egotistical, selfish ambition out of me like a doctor would
cut out a cancer. Beam your powerful love inside me and burn
it out. I want so much to be well, to be whole, to be the
somebody you want me to be. Help me, dear Lord!*

The chimes in the church began ringing. It was two
o'clock. I was supposed to be in the agent's office showing
how attractive I could be; instead, I was down on my knees
in my hotel room, and I'm sure I looked horrible. But as I
listened to the chimes, I felt strangely at peace with myself
and with God. A new source of power began to fill me, and

the glamour of screen tests — dressing rooms — stardom — began draining out of me.

I picked up my family's picture and looked into the faces of my babies. "Mommy's coming home," I whispered. "Mommy is coming home." I didn't know how I would get home, but I trusted God to get me there.

I called Paramount and got Bob Hope's dressing room. I left word asking him to call me. Then I called the coffee shop and got Olga.

"Olga, he didn't give me as much time as I thought he might."

"*He*? Mickey! Where are you? You're supposed to be at the agent's."

"God wants me to give it all up, Olga. I'm going home." I began choking up. "Thank you for everything, Olga. You'll never know what you've meant in my life."

"When are you leaving?"

"Right away, but I haven't checked the airlines."

"Listen, I'm going to call Arthur. We'll run you out to the airport."

I had finished packing when Bob returned my call.

"Mr. Hope, I'm terribly sorry, but I wasn't able to get out for the screen test. Something's come up. I'm leaving for home right away."

"What? Just as your dreams are about to come true? I wasn't just kidding. You've got the makings of a star. If you weren't going to follow through, why did you come out here?"

"I've — I've wanted a screen career more than anything in the world, but now I can't have it. My little girls are sick and crying for me."

"Oh, I see. Well, maybe you can get back out here later when you've made better arrangements for them."

"No, Mr. Hope, I won't be coming back. Tell Barney I'll write, and Mr. Hope, I'm sorry, I truly am."

"Listen, I'm holding things up here, but tell me, how are

you getting home? You indicated you didn't have much money to spare."

"Well, I need to fly."

"You find out the flight you want to take and call my secretary. When you get to the airline desk, your ticket will be waiting for you. Goodby, Mickey. And God bless you."

"Thank you, Mr. Hope. And God bless you."

Olga and Arthur took me out to the airport. I picked up my ticket and went to the designated gate. The plane was already loading. I hugged Olga and Arthur, then went out and climbed the ramp into the airliner. I was going home.

15

the talk of the town

When I arrived in Atlanta, I sent a telegram to Ollie at Camp Wheeler, in Macon, telling him that I was on my way home and would arrive in Macon by bus at 1 a.m. I didn't call because I felt I couldn't express my feelings over the phone.

On the bus, I gave a cold shoulder to the talkative lady next to me. I wanted to be alone with my thoughts. Although I was fearful that Ollie might not get my telegram in time, or might not be able to get a pass to meet me, I felt good inside. For half a dozen years there had been two persons inside my skin, vying to dominate my thoughts and behavior. Now there was only one person – Mickey Jordan, wife and mother. It seemed strange that God had been able to cut out so large a part of me and yet leave me feeling whole.

I rehearsed what I would say to Ollie. I would snuggle against his chest and say, "Ollie, darling, everything's going to be all right now. God has freed me from that dreadful compulsion to become a movie star, and I'm going to spend the rest of my life being a good wife to you and a good mother to Gayle and Sandra. I love you so very, very much. . . ."

And Ollie would kiss me and murmur in my ear, "Darling, this is the moment I've waited a lifetime for."

When I got off the bus, I saw Ollie waiting. The muscles in my legs and arms flexed to run to him and embrace him, but his face and stance signaled restraint. He didn't kiss me, nor did he say anything. As we waited for my luggage, I took his arm but felt no response. Finally, as he picked up my things, he said, "I've made reservations at the hotel across the street." "Good. I'm glad." I wanted to say more, but didn't.

Once in the hotel room, I threw my arms around Ollie. Crying uncontrollably, I forgot my neat little speech; instead, words just came tumbling out: "Oh, Ollie, say it's going to be all right. . . . I'll try awfully hard to be a good wife and mother. . . . I'll never leave you again, I promise."

Ollie stood with his arms down by his side. I looked up into his face, which was as rigid as his body. "Oh, Ollie!" I cried. "How can you do this to me?"

"Mickey," Ollie said, "you know I've loved you since the first time I laid eyes on you. I've worshiped the ground you've walked on ever since we married. But when you say you've given up your Hollywood dream – well, I just know you too well to believe that. You're like an alcoholic or a gambler – you can't quit. You want to be Mrs. Somebody, which is okay. But that would mean I'd be nothing more than Mrs. Somebody's husband. I couldn't move to Hollywood and just sit around. I sure couldn't open a farm equipment business at Hollywood and Vine."

I collapsed into a stuffed chair, put my head in my hands, and sobbed.

"Ollie, I ran off and left you and our babies, so you have a right to be angry with me. But try to put yourself in my shoes, too. They were ready to give me a screen test, and I turned my back on it and came home. I'm home to stay – you'll just have to believe it. I thought you'd be happy, but now I see you don't care."

Ollie wasn't going to believe me or forgive me. Now I wondered if I would ever forgive myself for giving up my big moment. I was left with only one place to go – home to Mother and Daddy.

I gathered up my suitcase, garment bag, and hat boxes. When I reached the door, I turned and looked back at him and said, "Ollie, please don't let me go, because if you do, I'll never come back again."

At this, he ran to me, grabbed my arms, and pulled me to him. "Oh, Mickey darling," he said, kissing my neck again and again.

I let go of my luggage and threw my arms around him and kissed him.

"Oh, Mickey, I don't know what to say."

"Don't say anything. Just hold me close."

"God has answered my prayers."

"*Your* prayers? Oh, Ollie, if you only knew how I prayed for God to make things right between us. Let's say he is answering both our prayers."

I was deliriously happy – and then the question struck me: Would Ollie have to go right back to camp? I was overjoyed when he said he had a three-day pass. I would have encouraged him to go absent without leave rather than have him leave me that night.

Early the next morning, we had breakfast and then headed for Henry Springs. Ollie told me about the new assignment he would have at Camp Wheeler following basic training, and I told him about my Hollywood adventure. He listened attentively. Now that Hollywood was no longer a threat to him, he was even able to laugh with me about some of my experiences.

After a period of silence, I said, "Ollie, there were roadblocks in my life so big that I couldn't move them out of the way, but God tore them down. I'm convinced there's nothing that God can't do if you give him the chance."

"I was just thinking the same thing."

"Ollie, we're going to be very, very happy."

We had a joyous reunion with our girls, stayed a couple of hours with my folks, then hurried home to spend the remainder of Ollie's pass together as a family. When the time had flown by, the girls and I drove Ollie back to camp.

I returned to Glendale with keen anticipation. I would pick up life where I had left off, only with enthusiasm. I would be a good housekeeper and mother, but I would also be efficient, thereby gaining free time in which to make friends and engage in community enterprises. Having a maid was a big help.

As a first step, I visited Gayle's Sunday School class. Her teachers seemed a bit cool, but I didn't think anything of it. I followed through on my intention to tell them I wanted to work in this class or some other class where I might be of service. They didn't seem overjoyed, but they promised to communicate my offer to the head of the children's division and the general superintendent.

The next day, I telephoned an order to the little delivery-service grocery a few blocks from our house. "Just charge that to my account," I said.

"I'm sorry, Mrs. Jordan," the proprietor said, "but we're having to pay cash for a lot of the things we buy these days, so if you don't mind, either give the delivery boy cash or your check."

I began to puzzle over the response of the Sunday School teachers and the grocery. Well, I would give the girls a tea party and invite some of their friends and their mothers. To my chagrin, the first child had "sniffles" and a second child's mother was "too busy." Suddenly, I recognized that something was very, very wrong.

I sat right down and called our pastor.

"People are acting as though I have the plague." I mentioned the Sunday School teachers, the grocer, and my neighbors. "People are talking behind my back. I want you to tell me what's going on."

The pastor cleared his throat. "I — I hardly know how to begin."

"Just begin at the beginning — anywhere. I can tell by your voice it isn't pleasant, but I'm asking you to help me."

"Mrs. Jordan, your husband's been away in the Army, you know. . . ."

"Yes, of course I know that. Go on!"

"Well, to put it bluntly, the word is that you went off to Atlanta with another man."

"That's ridiculous! I've been to Hollywood and I can prove it!"

"Mrs. Jordan, you don't have to prove it to *me*. And I don't think many of our people would repeat something like this. It'll blow over quickly."

"Oh, this is horrible! Please, you've got to help me tell people what really happened. I only went to Hollywood for a screen test. You can call Bob Hope for proof. Charge the call to my phone."

"That won't be necessary, Mrs. Jordan. I'll set the record straight whenever I hear anything — but I don't think I should bring the matter up, do you?"

"No, of course not, but please do whatever you can to stop these vicious rumors. I've acted selfishly and stupidly, but that's all."

I tried to resolve my conflicting feelings over how I should respond to this ugly talk. Should I pull out of the church and let them prattle, or should I slug it out? I decided that I shouldn't withdraw; indeed, the church ought to be the place where I would find comfort. I decided to go to the Wednesday night prayer service. My maid said she would stay with the children.

The sanctuary was abuzz, but when I walked in, it suddenly became quiet. People cast sidelong glances at me, then whispered to one another. During the service I sat alone, trembling with hurt and rage. I cringed when the pastor called for prayer concerns. If someone suggested prayers for me, I would be humiliated. But when no such suggestions were made, I became furious over the fact that some of these people had been wagging their tongues but obviously didn't care enough about me to pray for me.

When the service was over, I raced for the door. I ran out, climbed into my car, and sat there bawling. When I gained control of myself, I drove home.

I felt that my own church had rejected me and I swore I'd never darken its doors again. I wrote Ollie, demanding that he permit me to move to Davisville, Macon — anywhere. "If you were here," I pleaded, "I might be able to bear up, but with you gone, I'm not sure how much longer I can hold on." Ollie wrote back saying he was terribly sorry I was undergoing this embarrassment, but he was sure it would blow over soon. Hang in there without offending people unnecessarily, he urged. He would soon return to resume control of his business and would need all the friends he could get.

Humiliations continued. I heard nothing from my offer to work in the Sunday School, and even during the every-member canvass, nobody called on me. To avoid further embarrassment, I became a recluse. I ordered my groceries by phone and paid cash. I let the children walk to Sunday School instead of taking them. When a woman came to the door soliciting support of Castleberry College, which was in Glendale, I said, "I wouldn't be interested," and shut the door in her face.

One night, I was rushed to the hospital for an emergency appendectomy. My maid (what would I have done without her?) stayed with the children until Mother could come. Ollie arrived the next day on a three-day pass. During my two weeks in the hospital, none of the townspeople came to see me.

I was discharged and two days later developed adhesions and had to go back into the hospital for corrective surgery. Again, Ollie came home on a pass, and again I spent two weeks in virtual isolation.

I returned home too weak to look after Gayle and Sandra but nevertheless insisted that Mother go home. After a couple of days, I wrote Ollie, telling him I was near the end of my rope. Again, he promised he would be out of the service soon. He would come home and make things right.

Not long after that, I was awakened by a thunderstorm. The flashes of crackling lightning were immediately followed by house-shaking thunder. The night light in the bathroom went out, indicating a power failure. I lay there, frightened. I really didn't want to go back to sleep because I had been having nightmares which left me depressed the next morning.

The emptiness of my life weighed upon me, and the clock's minute hand seemed frozen. I had given up a chance for a movie career in order to be a good wife, a good mother, and a good citizen of the community, but I wasn't allowed the opportunity. And my husband either couldn't understand my desperate feeling or was unwilling to sell his business even if I lost my health and happiness, and perhaps my sanity. The future looked bleak, too. When he came home from the Army, he would again submerge himself in his work and have no time for me.

Suddenly, I sat up in bed and pulled out the drawer of my nightstand. As if in a trance, I groped for the handle of the pistol which was kept there. The cold steel was strangely inviting. I pulled back the hammer. I was astonished by the loudness of the click. At that moment, there was an explosion of thunder. The pistol would sound like that, I said to myself. The thought frightened me. In the same instant, Gayle called me from the children's bedroom. "Mommy! Mommy!"

"I'm right here, dear." Holding the pistol behind me, I groped my way into the kitchen and put the weapon on the topmost shelf. I didn't know how to release the hammer.

I felt my way into Gayle's room, took her in my arms, and rocked her. Her warm little body was comforting. She was so young, so dependent upon me. I began singing to her — songs that Papa Leslie had taught me — songs that she and her little friends had sung in Sunday School. "Jesus loves me, this I know, for the Bible tells me so. Little ones to him belong; they are weak, but he is strong." I laughed aloud when I recalled the time when Gayle mistakenly sang, "he is weak. but they are strong."

Jesus loved me, just as he loved this dear child in my lap. And if Jesus was for me, who could be against me? How did it go? "Neither heights, nor depths, nor devils, nor principalities can separate me from the love of God." I recognized that I hadn't quoted the verse correctly, but I was confident of its truth. If God was for me, who could prevail against me? Not all of the people of Glendale put together! *Oh, dear God, forgive me for almost committing a great sin. Forgive my sin of even thinking about it. And thank you for bringing me back from death to life. Take my life and use it for thy service. Amen.*

I was weary of mind and body, but I felt a sense of peace fall over me. God had eased my burden, just as he had that afternoon in the hotel in Los Angeles.

16

we enjoy the "good life"

My new, soft-green draperies and my carpet matched perfectly, and they combined with the red balls on the tree to fairly shout "Merry Christmas!" to our guests as they arrived. My hot seafood dip was heavenly, the eggnog had just the right zing, and the conversation was as bright as the candles burning on the dining room table.

On my way to the kitchen for more ice, I waltzed up to Ollie and put my mouth against his ear. "Ollie," I whispered, "I feel like I've really come back to life. With you home and with good friends to enjoy — well, all I can say is, it's the good life."

Since Ollie's discharge, we had clung to each other. He wanted to keep me happy so those old ambitions wouldn't flare, and I needed his love and attention to screen me from insults and to heal my hurts. He, too, resented the shabby way the people of Glendale had treated me, but we avoided a head-on confrontation with anyone. A squabble wouldn't have been good for Ollie's farm implement business, which was beginning to prosper again now that he was home. Instead of associating with established residents, we courted new and interesting couples who were moving into town as part of the postwar industrial boom. Most of these new friends were in top and middle management. They were well traveled, well informed, socially adept, witty, and charming. At least once a week, we got together with several other couples for cocktails and dinner. During the football season, we all went to Atlanta or Athens for a game and took a suite of rooms in a hotel or motel. We played cards a lot — at a tenth of a cent a point — and often we danced, which delighted me. I loved to dance. I also relished being the object of men's attentions. Ollie was a good dancer but had somehow featured himself clumsy on his feet. During our courting days, his reluctance to take me to public dances was a source of discord. Now we danced with our own, private set and Ollie felt comfortable about it — except when I flirted with the men. Ollie's jealousy showed, but he didn't make my coquettishness a big issue. He was too dedicated to keeping me happy and content.

Our "good life" included a comfortable, spacious house, two cars, chic fashions for me, and expensive suits for him. Ollie enjoyed providing for me and the girls, and the girls and I enjoyed what he provided.

Because we wanted the girls to have every advantage — and the advantages included Sunday School — one of us would drop them off, then come home to join the other in lounging and reading the Sunday paper. We talked about going to Sunday School and church, but two things deterred us: First, I still felt resentful toward my church (and decided the other churches in town would likely be just as gossipy); second, our Saturday night parties usually spilled over into the wee hours, so we just didn't feel like getting up and getting dressed on Sunday mornings.

Our parties got bigger, louder, and later — and our expenses grew larger, too. In my quieter moments, I sensed that my life was becoming emptier. I couldn't quite put my finger on what was wrong, but my doctor called it "anxiety neurosis."

We said grace at every meal (but never at our dinner parties, of course). Sometimes as I stood at the sink preparing the breakfast dishes for the dishwasher, I'd look out the window at our beautiful back yard and say a little prayer. It was always a prayer of thanksgiving rather than invocation — I didn't want to challenge God to wrestle with me over our need for spiritual growth. These were "the best years of our lives" and I didn't want them spoiled by pangs of conscience. We weren't doing anything really bad. Besides, we had experienced our share of rough seas, and surely God was willing for us to enjoy a few years of smooth, happy sailing.

Occasionally, my gnawing emptiness caused me to drop onto my knees and try to open myself up to God's voice, but I didn't concentrate very well. My mind soon wandered to mundane things — like figuring whether we ought to make it six couples instead of five — and would sherbet go better than pie with a heavy meal?

One afternoon, I had failed again at one of my on-my-knees seesions and had begun polishing the silver when the bell rang. The young woman at the door instantly reminded me of Olga — or was it someone else? Her face had classic lines and a "sweet" outlook. She gave her name and said she was calling in behalf of the Methodist church. I told her I didn't wish to pledge — that I thought I was putting my money to better use when I sent it to the little country church back home.

"Oh, Mrs. Jordan, I haven't come to *ask* for anything. I came to *give* something to you."

She reached into her purse and brought out a New Testament with mother-of-pearl covers.

"Bill and I made a trip to the Holy Land this spring and decided to buy ten of these testaments for relatives and friends. But Bill had a great idea. 'Henrietta,' he said, 'why don't we tithe with these testaments just as we do with our income? Let's buy an extra testament and put it away for a time when God wants us to use it.' We did, and here it is."

"Why, that's very sweet! I really don't know what to say."

"It's funny," she continued, "but I hadn't thought about the testament until this morning. The preacher called and said he had to go out of town unexpectedly, and he asked me to make several calls for him — two at the hospital and this one. He asked me to look in on you, inquire how you're getting along, and invite you and your family to our church."

I fingered the testament. "Well," I said, "it is really *our* church, too. Did the pastor mention that we're members?" "I don't remember; however, I don't think I've seen you there. Have I overlooked you?"

"Oh, no. Something happened and – well, we just haven't gotten back. Won't you come in?"

"No, I really didn't intend to impose. I know how inconvenient pop calls can be, although I sometimes wish people still dropped in unexpectedly, as they used to. I remember how much fun it was on Sunday afternoons when friends dropped in on our family back in Henry Springs."

"Henry Springs? I probably know your family. What was your maiden name?"

"Henrietta Mozeley."

"Then you're Grace Mozeley's little sister! Good heavens, Grace and I used to go round and round at each other. We had plenty of scraps."

"And you have to be Mickey Sauls! I had suspected it, but I didn't say anything, because I wanted to get off to a good start. Just the other day, Grace told me she hopes God has forgiven her for treating you so shabbily."

"Oh, that's over and forgotten. I heard that she married Durwood Johnston and they have a child."

"Three."

"The next time she's over here to see you, why don't you bring her by?"

"All right, I certainly will. . . . Mickey, you said something caused you to stop going to church."

God had sent Henrietta to me, but I didn't want to talk about the source of my hurt. "Let's just say some people said some untrue things that hurt me and I haven't found a way to forgive them."

"There's one sure way, and that's through Jesus Christ. Try it, Mickey. You and your family need the church and the church needs you. You have so much to give!"

"There *was* a time when I had something to give."

"But Mickey, you can make a new start. That's what the Christian faith is all about. You have the opportunity to clean the slate and begin anew."

"If you only knew how much I've wanted to erase my resentment, but just thinking about those hypocrites makes me ill. I want to forgive, but I can't."

She took my hands in hers. With the two of us standing in my doorway, she began to pray: "Lord, you know our deepest needs better than we ourselves do. You've heard Mickey's confession. Help her to find peace once again. We ask this in the name of our dear Savior. Amen."

Henrietta raised her head and looked into my eyes. "It's going to be all right now, Mickey," she said.

Her spontaneous prayer had taken me by surprise. I hardly knew what to say.

"Thank you so much, Henrietta. Come back soon. I want us to become better acquainted."

When I went into the house, my body seemed charged with electricity from the charisma of this young woman who had so beautifully shown me that she cared. And to think that she was Grace Mozeley's sister! God, how I had hated Grace. . . . *We've decided your eyes look like two fried eggs in a slop bucket. . . .* Once again, I could feel the principal's paddle cutting into my seat. . . . Grace had deliberately abused and humiliated me, *yet I had forgiven her, completely!* And by forgiving her, I had spared myself destructive feelings all these years. If I could forgive Grace, I could forgive *anybody.* I could and I would!

God, the hatred's all gone now. You've cut it out of me just as you cut that burning ambition out of me. I feel like a new person — fresh and clean. I've wiped the slate clean. I'm going to begin life anew, just wait and see.

Ollie and I began going to Sunday School with the girls, and soon we stayed regularly for church. I became a member of the Missionary Society and chancel choir. To my surprise, people accepted me. Either they, too, had decided to forgive and forget – or my imagination had built a bit of gossiping into a giant conspiracy. Either way, I was glad my ordeal was over.

One Sunday, the minister preached on God's call and man's response. God instructed Moses to go to Pharaoh and obtain release of the Israelites. Moses offered the excuse that he wasn't eloquent. God rejected this excuse, but to bolster Moses' courage, he said he would send along Aaron, who was a good talker; he also promised to put the right words into the mouths of both of them. Moses went, of course, and the Israelites were freed and God's will was done.

"Mickey Jordan," I said to myself, "all your life, you've been giving God excuses. You've refused his call again and again. One time you complain you didn't have a college education. Again, it's your being tied down with babies. Or your involvement in your own selfish little schemes – or your hurt because these little schemes have fallen through. It's a wonder that God has continued to love you, but he has. If he didn't love you, he wouldn't send one Moses after another to set you free. Just think of all those emissaries. There's been your own loving family, including Papa Leslie and Aunt Mary. There was Mildred in the detention center, Olga in the hotel, and now Henrietta in your church. And your patient, faithful, loving Ollie. You've been on the receiving end long enough. Now you drop those excuses of yours and go out into the world and witness to somebody else."

In a church which I had written off as being cold and cruel; in a town which I had despised; in a world which I resented for having inflicted hardships upon me – in this unlikely setting, I now found myself a redeemed person.

All my life, I had aspired to become a somebody. Now the glorious truth burst upon me: I was already a somebody – I had always been a somebody! My trouble was, I had been so busy drawing and revising my own blueprint that I had neglected to see and appreciate what God, the master builder, had already constructed – Mickey Sauls Jordan.

God's call became clearer and clearer to me, and I became more obedient – not perfectly obedient, but less rebellious. I had mistakenly thought he intended me to be the biggest frog in the biggest pond in the whole world, but now I recognized that he merely expected me to be a frog – but a creative, supportive, and loving one – in whatever pond I happened to find myself.

Having shaken off my false notions about my identity and destiny, and undergirded by his presence, I was able to spread my life in many directions where formerly I had neither the interest nor the talent. I directed plays, presented fashion shows, headed the PTA, supervised the recreation center, taught swimming. Glendale became "my town"; the people became "my people." They needed me and I needed them. Investing in others was good therapy. God took a swab dipped in tincture of love and healed those tender spots which had been festering deep within me all those years.

I was pretty proud of myself – until the day when the wife of the president of Castleberry College telephoned me. She was an engaging and gracious lady. We had a warm relationship – a personal thing that had nothing to do with Castleberry College, the *institution*, which I had never forgiven. In fact, I had done my best to ignore its presence in Glendale.

"Mickey," she said, "the reason for my call is that we want you to join our drama department."

"What? That's impossible. Didn't you know?"

"Didn't I know what, dear?"

"I got down on my knees and begged Castleberry College to give me a chance for an education, but I was refused because we didn't have money. I'm sorry if I sound bitter – but that's how I feel."

"Mickey," she said, warmly but firmly, "I want you to have lunch with me at the college tomorrow. I can understand how crushed you were. I can understand your lingering hurt. But I'm not going to let you continue to harbor this grudge against Castleberry because of what one person did to you, whether rightly or wrongly, so long ago — not if I can help it. You come out here and see what fine people we have on the staff and how eager our students are to learn — just as you were eager to improve yourself. Don't you see, Mickey, this is your opportunity to make things right. You can help these young people. Receipts from your productions can provide assistance to kids who otherwise would never have a chance for a college education. You've proved to this whole town that you're a pretty big person — I know. Let's have lunch tomorrow. Will twelve noon be okay?"

We had lunch together, of course. And, of course, I accepted the position. In the interim, God had made me acknowledge why I had held this old hurt to my bosom and nurtured it: Castleberry College's refusal was my excuse for not being as polished as I wanted to be. Its director of admissions was my excuse for not being somebody.

Our first play was *A Man Called Peter*. The afternoon before the performance, the girl who was to play Catherine Marshall became ill. We had no understudy, so I had to step into the role. We had rehearsed the play so thoroughly, I had unconsciously appropriated most of the lines.

The whole cast and crew performed marvelously. We could tell we had the audience with us — they laughed and cried, clapped and sat silent, always at the appropriate time. With the final curtain, the auditorium reverberated with applause. And during one of the curtain calls, I saw the president coming down the aisle with an armful of roses. When he presented them to me, I wept.

Later, as Ollie and I sat admiring those roses, I said, "Darling, that *was* a good play, wasn't it? But you know, the audience missed the real drama. The real drama was acted out on the stage of my heart."

17

god gives me a son

"Mother!" Gayle shouted as she came in from school. "Come and see the surprise I brought you."

The surprise was a handsome young man whose name, she said, was Leonard. He appeared a bit embarrassed. I was self-conscious, too, and wished Gayle wasn't so effusive on the occasion of this lad's first visit to our home.

"Mother, Leonard doesn't have a home. Can he live with us?"

On numerous occasions, Gayle and Sandy had brought in stray cats and dogs, but a homeless boy – that was right much.

"Stay with us?" I said. "Well, how long are we talking about?"

"Oh, Mother, I didn't say 'stay' with us – I said 'live' with us. You know, on and on, forever."

My daughter was serious! And she had put me on the spot. How many times had I begged the girls not to ask in their friends' presence whether they could eat with us or spend the night with us, and here my daughter was asking if this strange boy could live with us while he stood there shifting from one foot to another.

"Why, Gayle – Leonard – I don't know just what to say. Honey, we'll have to ask your daddy."

"I'm not worried about that," Gayle said. "He'll say yes if you do."

"We'll still have to wait and ask him," I said. "However, Leonard, you're welcome to stay and have supper with us."

"C'mon, Leonard," Gayle said. "I'll show you where your room will be."

In a little while, they joined me in the kitchen, and as I cooked, Leonard's story unfolded. As a baby, he had been left outside the door of an orphanage, where he lived until he was ten. He often tried to run away. He was placed in a foster home with an elderly couple who depended upon Leonard to do much of the work on their farm. He had fled this home at fifteen. Now, he was enrolled in our school and wanted to play football.

I drew Gayle aside.

"Honey, you don't just bring a boy home with you and ask your parents to let him live in your home. What's this all about?"

"Oh, Leonard's just a swell fellow who deserves a break. He's treated me nice at school, and now I want to do something for him. Besides, I'd love to have a big brother."

When Ollie came home, Leonard's history was related again.

"Daddy," Gayle said, "it just isn't right for some kids to have good homes and everything and other kids to go without."

While Leonard's eyes swept our nice dining room, Ollie's eyes swept Gayle, Sandy, and me.

"Leonard," he said, "we have rules about studying, bedtime, helping in the kitchen, making up beds — things like that. . . ."

"Yow-ee!" Gayle shouted, anticipating her father's yes.

"Could you live by our rules?"

"Yessir, I sure could."

"We'll try it then. You can move in tomorrow."

Leonard's eyes filled. "Thank you, Mr. Jordan. You won't be sorry."

I spent the next day converting our frilly guest room into a boy's room. I was just tidying it up when Gayle and her "brother" came home from school. Leonard tugged a beat-up suitcase.

"I tried to fix it up masculine-like," I said, "but you'll have your own ideas about pictures and pennants and things like that. We just want you to make . . ."

The expression on Leonard's face stopped me. It was a look of excitement tempered by incredulity. He sat down on the bed, bounced a couple of times, put out his hand to pat it, then stood and turned in a circle to get the entire effect.

"You know, I've never — I've never had a real room of my own before," he said, wiping tears from his eyes. "Mrs. Jordan, this is just beautiful, and so is your family. I promise I'll help you, and I'll study hard, and things like that."

I had to turn away, I was so choked up. After all these years, God had sent me a son. A half-grown son who was still struggling desperately to be somebody. In that moment, I recognized that he and I had a lot in common. We would get along very well.

That night, as we all got up from the supper table, Leonard said, "I'd like to ask you a question."

"Sure, Leonard," Ollie replied.

"Can I call you Mother and Daddy?"

"You sure can," Ollie and I said in unison, hugging him.

I like to think we contributed a lot to Leonard's young life; certainly he enriched our lives. For one thing, he reminded us not to take our many blessings for granted.

The first Christmas that Leonard was with us, our tree was, as usual, practically afloat with gifts. I had seen to it that our new son had more presents than anyone else. When the first was placed in his lap, he fingered the card and said, "Mother, until now I've never had a Christmas present with my name on it." As he opened each gift, he ran to us and thanked us.

It seemed strange having a son, but in a way it seemed that he had always been with us. Ollie enjoyed Leonard and understood him. At one point, Leonard wanted a motorcycle. I objected; I was afraid he would kill himself. But Ollie took Leonard to a shop sixty miles away and bought him a cycle.

"On the way home, I was afraid the kid was going to get a crick in his neck," Ollie said. "He never took his eyes off that bike in the back of the pickup."

Leonard's exposure to religious training had been spotty, and I worked diligently to help him; in the process, I helped myself. It was good for me to be concerned with someone else's spiritual life. Oh, I had done this with the girls, but their questions and concerns hadn't come to me full-blown as Leonard's did.

In retrospect — what with today's attention to legalities — it seems strange that Leonard "just lived with us," but that was the case. I suppose the authorities were aware of his being with us and were glad the boy had a good home.

One day, an old couple drove up in a truck that was, as we used to say, "held together with hay-baling wire." The couple was just as rickety. The Santa Claus-like old gentleman assisted his wife, who was wearing a long apron and a huge sun bonnet, and who walked with a cane.

"Me'n Pa's come a fur piece to see ya," she said to me. "Both of us is sick and we wanted to git here 'fore we taken and died. We jist don't want ter die without y'all knowin' yer th' answer to our prayers."

They were the foster parents from whom Leonard had run away. They were heartbroken over his leaving them, yet they didn't blame him.

"Two old folks like me'n Pa don't have no business tryin' to raise a young'un," Miss Pearl said.

Every night she and Pa had prayed for God to lead Leonard to a good home. Satisfied that their prayers had been answered, they insisted on getting back into their ancient vehicle and proceeding home. They were content, they said, and they didn't want to upset Leonard with their presence.

I gave them a picture of Leonard and assured them that Leonard often spoke kindly of them.

As the old rattletrap clattered away, I said a prayer for the old couple's safety and welfare. I appreciated their coming to tell me something that I already knew: It was God who had sent me my son.

My life was never one of moderation. Most of it was a rollercoaster ride – ecstatic climbs followed by abysmal plunges – but always with the throttle wide open. Now I was in a "level" period of total investment in my family and in community betterment projects, but this didn't mean I had slowed down; to the contrary, I was roaring across this plateau as a racer would streak across the salt flats of Utah.

"What are you trying to prove?" my doctor asked. "You've got to slow down or you'll kill yourself."

His scolding fell on deaf ears. Now that I was somebody, I didn't want to say no to an invitation whether it was for a social affair or a demanding job. My family needed me and my community needed me – and I needed to be needed. I began finding myself too tired to go to sleep and too tired to get up. Obviously my body – which had borne the brunt of years of tensions, conflicts, and relentless drive – was signaling me to slow down.

Gayle graduated from Rollins College one day in June, then became a radiant bride the next day. I managed to attend the graduation and wedding. A week later, I collapsed.

I was taken by ambulance to Piedmont Hospital in Atlanta. At first, the doctors suspected coronary heart disease; however, tests, x-rays, and closer examination produced a diagnosis of double hiatal hernia – protrusions through the esophagus' passageway through the diaphragm.

Surgery was ordered. Having had seven operations already, this wasn't a new experience for me, and I wasn't afraid. A hard-driving woman of forty-three wasn't likely to die in surgery, was she?

The operation took three hours, followed by five hours in the recovery room. At this point, the doctors told Ollie I was doing well and advised him and the rest of the family to go to the hotel and get some rest.

Later that night, Ollie and the family were summoned. "We're doing everything we can for her," a doctor said. "We haven't been able to stabilize the functioning of her heart and lungs." While the doctors and nurses worked frantically to save my life, Ollie, Gayle, and Sandra (Leonard was in Paris with the Air Force) prayed, using waiting room chairs as altars.

Amid the swirl of activity, I felt detached. It seemed that I was outside myself, viewing what was happening. I felt no pain and no fear. At one point, I asked for Ollie and they let him come in and slip his hand under the oxygen tent and hold my hand briefly.

"Don't worry, darling," he said.

Minutes after he went out, a quiet fell upon the room as though it were filling with downy snowflakes. I dozed, then opened my eyes. Beyond the circle of doctors and nurses stood Jesus. His robe was dazzling white and his face was even more radiant. He held his arms out wide as if to invite me to come to him. My immediate reaction was to cringe, for I felt terribly guilty – unworthy to be in his presence. As I continued to look into his pleading face, I silently vowed to seek a better life. He smiled a warm, tender smile. I sensed he was saying everything would be all right. Then he disappeared.

Promptly, I felt a surge of strength, and I heard someone say, "She's better!" I looked up and saw relief written in the faces above me. Then I drifted into a deep and peaceful sleep.

When I awoke, I was cheered to find Ollie with me. A couple of days later, my whole family was able to come in together. There was an outpouring of cards, letters, telegrams, and flowers.

When I learned that our new pastor, the young and dynamic Rev. Reece Turrentine, had asked members of the church to pray for me during and following my surgery, I immediately connected this prayer vigil with Christ's appearance to me. However, I didn't mention my seeing Jesus for some time; I was afraid people – perhaps even Ollie –

would dismiss my experience as having been a dream or hallucination.

My discharge brought tearful goodbys with the lifesaving team and others who had cared for me. When the ambulance finally reached Glendale, the nurse who accompanied me pulled back the curtains for me to glimpse the grand old courthouse. Soon I was in that wonderful bed of my own.

When I had been home a few days, I told Ollie about Jesus visiting me.

"Do you believe me?" I asked.

"I do. I certainly do."

"Ollie, I have to start living for Christ," I said. "I want us to give him complete charge over our lives."

Ollie agreed, and in that moment, we surrendered ourselves anew to Jesus.

Ollie and I had long recognized the need to reorient our lives, but we hadn't shared this concern. We didn't want to jeopardize the "good life." We both enjoyed our parties, cocktails, and exclusive mutual-admiration clique. Ollie enjoyed his weekly night out with the boys, playing nickel and dime poker over a beer or two. These were good friends; he didn't want to abandon them, insult them, or have them think he had turned into a goody-goody sort of person. My confrontation with Jesus brought our individual apprehensions and longings into the open, leading us to our resolve to pursue a new and better life.

The conversion was easier than we had expected. When we surrendered our lives to Jesus Christ and permitted ourselves to be immersed in his love, things began falling in place.

Ollie and I began starting and ending our days in prayer. As we went our separate ways, we noted people's concerns and together lifted up these concerns in prayer. We attended church services regularly and assumed larger roles of leadership. For example, I became a member of the official board. All of this brought us closer together in our marriage.

"You know, life really does begin at forty — add or subtract a few years," Ollie said one Sunday afternoon as we drove home from visiting the sick and shut-ins. "I think we're turning into nuts of some kind."

"We're getting a little wacky," I said, sliding over against him, "but I love it."

Mornings after Ollie left for work, I read my Bible, reflected, and planned toward the future. Perhaps because of my harsh childhood and later disappointments, the scripture that kept coming to me was the affirmative query, if God is for me, who can be against me? Unfortunately, I hadn't discovered the deeper truth of this passage. I had been closer to its meaning when I pushed aside my hurt and plunged into church and community activities than during this later period of spiritual tranquility. Now I assumed that God always protects his own from any kind of hurt.

My faith was soon to be tested again.

18

miracles still happen

Ollie's business was such a thriving enterprise that we assumed it would prosper forever. We were shaken when two circumstances began conspiring against it. One was a business recession, which sharply curtailed capital expenditures. The other was increased participation in the government soil bank — farmers were paid for letting fields lie fallow.

Ollie found himself selling fewer and fewer tractors and other equipment. He was caught with an enormous inventory. And his customers owed him large sums of money — money they couldn't pay. Ollie, in turn, couldn't satisfy his own creditors.

At first, we felt that this economic cloud would soon blow over. Farming was so much a part of us and our rural community. Besides, we were praying to God. God loves us. He would make things right again.

It didn't work out that way. Month by month, I helplessly watched Ollie's business slip through his hands as sand sifts through one's fingers.

In my panic, I asked God for a miracle. *Don't let Ollie fail. He's too good, too honest — he's worked too hard — people need his fair deals and good service. He deserves better. And what about me? Haven't I surrendered my life? God, you don't want us to suffer! Give us a miracle!*

If God was listening, he didn't indicate it. The only thing we could thank him for was our new life-style, which had reduced our expenditures for food, beverages, flowers, and gifts. Each week, we tightened our purse strings.

Ollie worked day and night. He sought extensions of credit from his suppliers and new loans from financial institutions. Finally, it became untenable to continue the business. Going on meant digging the grave a little deeper.

Friends, including fellow businessmen, urged Ollie to file a petition of bankruptcy. He was a victim of circumstances, they said. He had slaved to keep his business solvent. To lose it was punishment enough; he shouldn't continue to carry an impossible indebtedness, they argued.

"I can't take that way out," Ollie said. "I'm going to pay off my creditors if it takes me the rest of my life. I don't know how, but I'll do it."

I couldn't advise Ollie. I could only listen — and love him.

I'll never forget the morning that Ollie closed his business. It hurt me to see his shoulders dragging the ground as he left the house. He had only to pack his books and papers and lock the doors. Yet, it would be the hardest task of his life.

I was straightening the house when it occurred to me that I ought to be with Ollie. But when I got there, I found the place locked. Ollie's car was gone. I was frightened. He had been so depressed. I didn't know where to look for him, and I didn't want to call around and alarm friends. Ollie probably had gone to the cafe for coffee, or to the bank, or maybe for a little ride to be alone with his thoughts.

About an hour later, Ollie pulled into our driveway and I ran out to meet him. His eyes were red, but he gave me a soft, sweet smile.

"It's okay," he said. "I talked with God about it and it's okay. When I closed up, I drove over to the church. It seemed the place to go. In that quiet sanctuary, I told God how much I hurt — as if he didn't already know. I told him I wanted to be a man about it; I wanted to do his will. God told me he loves us, and he's going to be with us all the way. I guess I was hoping for an easy answer, but I didn't get one – just his promise to love us."

Ollie choked up. I massaged his shoulders and said, "You know, I married a bigger man than I suspected."

"It's going to be all right, baby," he said. "I feel sure of it."

"Of course it will," I said. Isn't that what a wife's supposed to do – be bright and cheerful even though she doesn't see a glimmer of sunshine on the whole brooding horizon? As I poured us a cup of coffee, I wondered how God was going to handle this one.

I should have known that one of God's responses would be to send some wonderful people to share our hurt and point us in the right direction.

One of God's emissaries was the Rev. Ben Johnson, now director of the Institute of Church Renewal in Atlanta, but then pastor of the First Methodist Church in Phenix City, Alabama. At the invitation of Reece Turrentine, Ben came to our church to organize groups which were to practice some innovative prayer methods he had designed. In our first general meeting, I was immediately captured by this winsome combination of country boy and erudite theologian. I knew he had to be as big of heart as he was of stature, so when he announced that he would be in the church office for counseling in the afternoon, I knew I would be there.

"I'm Mickey Jordan," I said upon entering.

"Yes, I remember you. This morning I somehow got the communication that you'd be coming."

I poured my heart out and went home renewed.

"He knew just what to say," I told Ollie that evening, whereupon it dawned on me that Ben had said very little. What he had done was to give me an attentive and supportive ear. He had permitted me to spill out my hopes, fears, hurts, aspirations – everything. Then he had led me to identify which issues of my life were worth concern and which were not. This accomplished, I set some priorities. The result was finding a path where I had previously been stumbling about.

I had learned a principle of counseling which would be extremely helpful later as I sought to help other persons. Ben asked me to come to Phenix City the next Sunday night and share my witness with his congregation. It was a frightening prospect, but I couldn't refuse. One of my priorities was to tell other people how God had come into my life and blessed me.

As I began my talk, I found myself clutching the pulpit. I looked down at Ben, who was giving me a you-can-do-it smile, and I knew he was praying for me. Then I looked out over the congregation. They were people just like me – people with hurts and disappointments. The only thing I had to give to them was myself. I opened up my heart to them, and their response was gratifying.

The prayer groups which Ben organized and Reece and his wife, Onie, nurtured brought our church into a spiritual revival. Ollie and I became members of a group which was like a family. One night, I told them about our concern for our future. I asked for their prayers – which they immediately gave.

Ollie and I were getting ready for bed when the doorbell rang. To our surprise, there was Ted Norton, a member of the prayer group, in pajamas and a robe.

"You were on my heart and I couldn't sleep," Ted said. We invited him in.

"I want to help any way I can. I'd like to lend you some money – or give it to you if you'll accept it."

We didn't accept Ted's money, but we accepted his love. It meant more to us than pure gold.

Several weeks passed and Ollie was becoming discouraged. Nobody around Glendale needed his specialized skills and experience, and nobody wanted to hire him in a lesser capacity for fear he would soon become dissatisfied. He really couldn't afford to take a low-paying job on a permanent basis – he'd never clear up his debts.

Then one day I came home from an errand and found Ollie quite excited over a phone call from a large Atlanta tractor company offering him a job. Since he hadn't contacted them, their offer came as a complete surprise.

"They're giving me southeast Georgia, baby! Isn't it wonderful?"

"It's more than just *wonderful*," I said. "It's a miracle!"

With Ollie traveling, I was alone much of the time. One Sunday evening after Ollie got off on an all-week trip, I visited my friend Dorcas Gambill.

"I want you to go to Florida with me this week for an ashram," she said.

"An *ashram*? What in the world is that?"

"It's a spiritual retreat. People from all over come together to pray, study, and share the Lord's blessings. The resource person will be Rosalind Rinker. You'll fall in love with her."

Two days later, I found myself in an auditorium listening to Rosalind Rinker's introductory remarks. Several women accepted her invitation and described their personal journeys along the road of faith. I envied their composure and ability to articulate their stories.

Suddenly, I found myself on my feet. The assembly gazed at me expectantly; they assumed that I, too, would give an account of my Christian experience. Instead, I said, "I am seeking a closer walk with God. Please pray for me." Then I sat down.

When the session closed, Rosalind came straight over to me. She had been touched by my simple plea and wanted us to find a quiet place where we could talk.

God told me to open up and describe my most urgent concerns — even my ugliest side — to Roz. If you've read any of Roz's books, you know she's an expert on prayer. We prayed together and she led me to a closer relationship with my Savior.

"I want what she has," I said to myself. "I want to open my life completely to God's guidance."

When I got home, God led me to seek out a job and help Ollie with that enormous debt. Gayle was married, Leonard was in France, and Sandy was away in college, so I felt free to pursue full-time employment. I lacked impressive credentials — no college degree, very little actual experience, and my typing and shorthand were rusty. In Glendale, there were few jobs for women and fewer still that paid well.

Lord, I need a job. You've given Ollie a new career and we're thankful for that, but I need to help him. Frankly, Lord, I need a job that will pay good money — more than I'm making teaching drama — and if I'm not asking too much, I'd like to use my talent for moving about and meeting people — maybe something in public relations.

Ollie had no idea I was job-seeking until I read him an ad in the Sunday paper:

"Large national concern needs woman to travel southeast as a cosmetics consultant. Good appearance, speaking ability required. Excellent pay, generous fringe benefits."

"I just might apply," I said.

"Well, why don't you?" Ollie responded.

I wrote to the company and soon received a special delivery letter setting up an appointment in Atlanta.

In the interim, I was to meet Roz for an ashram, again in Florida. Roz and I shared a room, and that weekend we turned my job concerns over to God.

"Father," Roz prayed, "if this is to be Mickey's job, give her the poise she needs for the interview. Take away her anxiety — help her to go to her interview knowing that if she isn't to get the job, it's because you have something better for her to do." How different from my own aggressive approach!

"But Roz," I said, "how can I be confident looking like this? I won't even have time to get an appointment with my hairdresser."

"Pray about it," Roz said. "Chances are somebody will cancel and you can have her appointment."

And that's what happened.

When I arrived at the hotel suite for my interview, I was

dismayed to find the waiting room filled with applicants. "Never mind," I said to myself. "If the job's to be yours, you'll find the resources to compete."

When my name was called, I walked into the inner room with an air of quiet confidence.

"Why, you look like a movie star," the poised and attractive lady said, giving me a warm handshake.

For the next half hour, she and I sat and chatted over cups of coffee. She didn't seem to be in a hurry, and I certainly wasn't in a rush. When I became fearful I might be imposing and rose to leave, she picked up the phone and called her New York office.

"I've found my Atlanta girl!" she said.

And I said to myself, "Chalk up another miracle for God."

do good to those who hate you

God not only answered my prayer for a career — he gave me a glamor job. I traveled the Southeastern United States giving four-hour lecture-demonstrations to cosmeticians. I was part of the beauty industry, which challenges women to be up to the minute in grooming and dress — ready for anything! Naturally, I stayed up on my own toes, too.

At the outset, I recognized that it was an exhausting job. Sunday afternoons, I drove to Columbus, where I caught a plane either that night or early the next morning for the first city on my itinerary. Friday afternoons, I flew back into Columbus and drove home. Yet, for several years, I was ecstatic about my job. There were so many advantages — such as meeting interesting, exciting people. And, more importantly, I had numerous opportunities to share my Christian witness with these people.

I became a close friend of a buyer for one of the larger department stores in the South. Outwardly, she was the epitome of the beautiful, sharp, confident woman executive. Inwardly, she was troubled. She had become entangled in so many extramarital affairs that even she couldn't keep track of them, and finally her husband left her. She remarried, whereupon her sister ran off with her new spouse. Now she was estranged from her whole family.

One evening, following my lecture, I sensed she was especially low, so I said, "C'mon Carol, I'll buy you a steak."

I took her to a nice restaurant and insisted that we have a steak. Carol picked at her food. Soon she was crying.

"I can't eat, Mickey," she said, laying down her fork. "How can I eat when my life is in such a mess?"

"I'll find you some help," I said.

Leaving our steaks virtually untouched, I led Carol out of the restaurant.

"Where are you taking me?" she asked. "If you're thinking about a psychiatrist, I've already got one of those. And preachers don't do any good."

"I'm taking you to somebody who can make things right," I said.

We walked down the street. Entering the first church we came to, we went down to the altar and dropped onto our knees.

"God," I prayed, "listen to Carol, one of your children. She needs your help. . . ."

She remained silent.

"Just talk to him, Carol — like you would your own father."

"I can't pray," she sobbed, "because I can't accept God as a father. My own father ditched my mother and me when I was two years old."

"Then talk to Jesus as you'd talk with me or any other friend," I said, putting an arm around her.

"But I've never prayed out loud before in my life," she protested.

Two hours later, when we left the church, God had changed Carol's life. And once again, he had deeply touched my own life.

Another time, while waiting to board a plane, I prayed, "Dear Father, let me sit next to someone who needs a sympathetic ear and a Christian witness."

I went aboard and took a seat. Soon a rumpled little old lady came along and plopped down beside me.

"Praise the Lord!" she said. "I almost missed the plane.

As I scooted through the terminal, I prayed that God would put me next to somebody who needed my witness. You must be the one."

For the next hour, this little woman gave the most joyous — and funniest — witness I've ever heard. I had no chance to tell her that God had played one of his divine jokes on the two of us — in fact, I never got a word in edgewise.

My mother used to say that Aunt Mary taught me to sprinkle dynamite on my eggs instead of pepper. On my job, I was the same compulsive, hard-driving person that I was before. Now, when I look back on the eight and one-half years I spent traveling for the cosmetics company, I marvel that I didn't experience either a fatal stroke or a nervous breakdown. I was a week-long executive and a weekend wife. I had been in the job only a couple of years when I recognized there would never be enough time for either role. This left me frustrated, but unwilling to surrender. As my frustrations mounted, I attempted to drown them in frenzied activity. Again, my body underwent severe punishment.

I became jealous of my time. If we lived in Atlanta, I thought, that would save five or six hours' traveling time each week — half a dozen hours that I could invest in my marriage, my family (we now had four grandchildren), my church, and my community. I talked to God about this problem and possibility, but I was always constrained to add, "But Lord, I recognize how much Ollie's job means to him. I don't want to interfere with his work. Simply give me strength to deal with my own situation."

One Saturday morning, I found so many chores and errands facing me, I decided to make a list. I quickly jotted down eight or ten tasks. Then I whimsically wrote at the bottom of the list, "Love Ollie." As I gazed at that entry, the humor drained out of it. All too often, I really was putting my husband last.

I knew I ought to add still another item: "Do something for my church." Nowadays, it was impossible for me to take leadership roles. About once a month, I traveled to some host church, where I joined other guests in a sharing ministry, but these trips weren't connected with my own local church. I felt the void all the more acutely because I had previously been so very active — and so very rewarded. Now I almost dreaded going to Sunday School or morning worship because somebody was bound to make a pitch for broader participation by the congregation.

One Sunday, the lesson was on investing your talents versus burying them. In that particular teacher's mind, there was only one place of investment that counted — the church. I went home feeling guilty, and I carried the guilt with me all that week.

Well, I wouldn't get my chores done sitting there. I glanced at the clock. I had twenty minutes in which to get a bath, get dressed, and keep my appointment with my hairdresser.

I was walking out the door when a car drove up. It was Henrietta's car, and the woman getting out of it had to be — yes, it was — Grace Mozeley! Grace was a pretty teen-ager and she never wanted for clothes, but I was unprepared for what I saw. This woman was strikingly handsome. She had an elegance about her. She instantly communicated poise.

Henrietta waved to me and called something about having to run an errand and then she'd return and join us.

I threw my arms around Grace and said, "I'm so glad to see you." I was — and I wasn't. I had wanted to sit down and assure Grace that, as far as I was concerned, everything was okay between us. But my appointment and the rest of my list flashed upon the screen of my mind, and I wished Grace hadn't come.

"Mickey," Grace said, "you're as beautiful as ever." I felt an impish urge to say, "Yeah, like two fried eggs in a slop bucket," but I didn't. Instead, I said, "Come on in, sit down, and tell me all about yourself." I added, "I'll fix us a cup of coffee," because I had to have the opportunity to call my hairdresser and tell her I would be late.

By the time we had drunk our second cup of coffee, we

had exhausted every *pleasant* experience we had shared. I wished Grace would say something about how mean she had been so that I could tell her I had completely forgiven her. I didn't think I should bring the subject up, since I had been the victim. Occasionally, Grace exhibited an anxiousness which suggested there was something she wanted to talk about but couldn't.

Finally, I said, "Grace, you're holding something back on me and I think I know what it is. It's those hassles we got into back in school."

"No, Mickey, it's not that at all. You've been so warm to me, I've just known that you've forgiven me, and I pray that God has forgiven me. Lord knows, I've prayed about it dozens of times."

"Then what is it, Grace?"

"Well, it's a long story, and I don't think I should burden you with it."

I quickly debated whether I should plead a busy schedule and ask Grace to defer her confession or say I had all the time in the world. I chose the second alternative.

"You know, Mickey, I married young. I was only eighteen. I wasn't, as they say, 'over fool's hill yet' — in fact, I hadn't even climbed it. Durwood was a nice, good-looking, hardworking guy, but I kept wondering if I really wanted to spend the rest of my life with him — with him alone, that is. We had our first child right away, and I felt more trapped than ever."

"I know what you mean," I said.

"There was a boy I'd been in school with — you'd know him if I called his name. I got him over to the house on the pretext of giving me an estimate on some repair work, and I literally seduced him. I thought this was a way for me to test whether I really loved Durwood. Naturally, the affair didn't end with this first episode, but it didn't take me long to see that this extra relationship was leading me nowhere, fast! Both of us — maybe all of us — were going to get hurt. So I broke away from this second man.

"But Mickey, I didn't break away soon enough. Word about this thing had spread all over town. One night I confessed to Durwood. He said he already knew. He also said he still loved me. I knew for sure, then, that there was only one man for me — Durwood — and I vowed to devote my life to making him happy. Still, I had this blot on my conscience — just like the blot from treating you so bad. I prayed to God about it, and I thought I heard him saying I should become active in the church, but I soon found that the church didn't want me.

"We had two other children in quick succession. Durwood had to take a moonlighting job. I felt terribly lonely, especially at night. And during the day, I felt that my family was draining my personhood out of me. Oh, they weren't especially demanding — it just takes a lot of doing to keep a household of five going."

I started to break in and tell her something of my own story, or to begin making suggestions, but I recognized she might not be through, and certainly she hadn't asked what she wanted of me.

"I also had to help look after mother. She has cancer, you know."

"No, I didn't know. Henrietta didn't mention that."

"Oh, Henrietta wouldn't. To listen to her, there's no sickness, no evil in the world. I kid her, saying she'd make a good Christian Scientist. She's a dear and I love her, but I can't talk to her about my deepest concerns — she sort of dismisses them as though they weren't there. You know what I mean? I find it hard to relate to somebody like that. I hurt, and I have to tell somebody about my hurt."

"I'm like that, too," I said.

"Mickey, I'm still wrestling with guilt from cheating on Durwood. But at the same time, I feel I have a lot to offer. I can understand people's problems better because of my own experience. I feel that I ought to be able to relate to people who are hurting, because I've hurt so much myself."

"And you've come to me because you've heard I've had some jolts in my life, too."

"No, Mickey, I came to you because God sent me. You have something that I need. I suppose that, in a way, our past difficulties also influenced my coming. You know, there's one of our children who's given us the most trouble, and would you believe he's the one we feel closest to? Mickey, I do feel close to you."

"I'm glad, Grace. I really am."

"But the main reason I came is, as I said, because you have something you can give me. I know you've been going to other churches telling about your spiritual experiences. I want to be able to share like that."

"Well, if today's any indication, I'd say you could do a good job of it — although you may or may not wish to be quite so explicit."

"But that's just it, Mickey. I don't think I can do a good job of it. I've never been able to get up before a group and say what I want to say and need to say. I've never had your flair for public speaking or dramatics or things like that."

"I don't know whether I could help, but would you like for me to try?"

"I sure would," she said, and I could tell by the promptness of her response that, at last, I had come to the point of her visit.

I agreed to work with her the next three Saturdays. Where the time would come from, I didn't know, but I felt God's urging that I go it on faith.

"Before you go, Grace, I want to make an observation and then I want to ask your help with something."

"Okay."

"First, don't feel that you're the only person who's been tempted to step outside his or her marriage. I'm on the road all week, staying in hotels and motels. Sometimes in the evening as I dine alone, the music coming out of the lounge sounds awfully sweet. I love to dance, and it's mighty hard for me to go back to my room and risk having the walls close in on me, as they often do. There's always some man who asks to join me at my table, or asks me to have a drink with him — even to have a nightcap with me in his room or my own. Sometimes these guys are pure pests and I'm glad to shake them; at other times, especially when I'm lonely, they seem so nice and friendly. We all have these feelings at times, I think. In my case, I have to recognize that the devil is at work; he's tempting me to let my *old self* creep in. I've prayed about this with Reece and Onie — my pastor and his wife. Reece gave me a good suggestion: 'When some guy invites you to have dinner or a drink with him, tell him you'll be happy to meet him for breakfast, instead.' You know, it works."

"That's a clever idea."

"Now, you give me some counsel. As I say, I'm gone all week. Ollie travels, but when he's home, he's to himself. I come in Friday evening and find a dozen things demanding my time. . . ."

"Oh, Mickey, I shouldn't be imposing upon you!"

"No, Grace, that's all right, really. But to get back to my problem, I find all these things to do. The result is, I don't feel that I have enough time for my husband. You had this problem and you seem to have solved it. What's your secret?"

"It's simple. When I'm with Durwood, I'm with him one hundred percent."

I met with Grace the next several Saturdays and helped her with her diction, gestures, stage presence, and so forth. And she continued to help me discover ways to enrich my marriage, as well as other areas of my life.

It was, as Grace suggested, simpler than I had realized. The key to relating to Ollie or any other human being was to *really be with them* instead of relating to them casually. Ollie and I had made commitments to our jobs and to paying off our debts. We could throw these commitments over, or we could live with them. God had given us these jobs, knowing the problems they involved, and God would help us fulfill them. I know that our marriage wouldn't have prevailed if it hadn't been for God's hand in our lives.

Grace's little principle helped me in resolving my feelings about my church activities, too. Now I recognized that my job enabled me to be with people. This, it seemed to me, was what persons were desperately seeking — someone to take them and their situations seriously — listen to them — earnestly try to help them to find their best options. And, above all, to remind them that God loves them.

A few months after Grace and I got reacquainted, Ollie's company was acquired by a larger firm and we moved to Atlanta. Again, God seemed to be at work in the world and in our lives. I recaptured that half a dozen hours a week that I had spent getting to a plane.

I rarely see Grace now, but I often reflect upon the storybook character of our relationship. Nobody but Grace could have helped me at that particular time toward working out my problems, and, more importantly, coming to a higher understanding of myself. For all my faults, I wasn't as bad as I had thought. A child who battled those who did her wrong had grown into a woman who could forgive. A woman who was wracked with guilt and feelings of inadequacy had become able to give of herself — the greatest thing that she *could* give.

20

healed by
the great physician

I'm an Aries, born under the sign of the Ram. My zodiacal sign is appropriate, because I've always tried to butt my way through life.

Often, God speaks to me, saying, "Be still and know that I am God." He warns that I'm going to miss life if I keep trying to race through it. Sometimes I listen (more often now than in the past); sometimes I either pretend not to hear or act as though I were wiser than God. There have been times when it seemed the only way God could command my attention was to get me flat on my back. Medical problems have been a large part of my life. I've already mentioned my operations following the birth of my girls, and my hiatal hernia episode, when Jesus appeared in my hospital room.

I remember another occasion, a rainy winter day. On my way to see my doctor, I felt I was in trouble. Several weeks earlier, I had noticed a small lump in my right breast. Although I had been through a cancer scare once before, I delayed seeing the doctor. I didn't want to go through another operation − besides, it probably was just a clogged duct. Within three weeks, however, the knot was too large to ignore.

My fears were confirmed when my doctor, having examined me, strode briskly out of the room with a worried look on his face.

"Let's get dressed," the nurse said cheerily. I was trembling so I couldn't find the buttonholes in my blouse. As I waited for the doctor, I heard him in his office talking to the hospital.

"Yes, I need to get her in as soon as possible. A biopsy of the breast. That's fine. Thank you."

The doctor came back into the examining room. He said he felt he ought to operate right away to determine whether or not the lump was malignant.

"I've scheduled you to enter the hospital day after tomorrow. Is that all right?"

On the way home, the word "cancer" stabbed into my consciousness like an icy dagger tearing into my heart. What if the doctor had to do a radical mastectomy? How would Ollie feel? How would I feel about myself? My windshield fogged over. I tried to wipe it clear, then gave up. My future was just as unclear as the piece of glass.

When I reached the house, I picked up my cat. "Ellie," I whispered, "I'm in bad trouble. I dread telling Ollie. I even dread hearing him call, 'Baby, I'm home!' "

When Ollie came, he gathered me in his arms and put his face against mine. I struggled to find the courage to tell him.

He looked into my brimming eyes and said, "I know. The doctor called me."

The morning of my surgery, I was serene. I went to the operating room secure in the knowledge that members of several prayer groups were at that moment praying for me, using lighted candles as points of concentration.

Lord, I give you my body. Do with it what you will. And, Lord, if I weaken and try to back away from you, don't pay any attention to these lapses. Just know that I trust you and am reconciled to your will.

Many hours later, I became aware of Ollie's presence. He was stroking my forehead and saying, "It's all right, baby. Everything is fine."

I frantically felt for my breasts. They were both there!

"Oh, Ollie," I exclaimed. "Thank the Lord!"

Although Christ was not visible in this instance, I felt that he had been with me just the same. There followed a period in which I pondered the questions that Christians have asked for two thousand years: Are all things possible for those who truly believe? Do I believe God is all-powerful, or half powerful? Curiosity led me to read Kathryn Kuhlman's books on miracles, and when I heard that Miss Kuhlman was coming to Atlanta to hold a miracle service in the auditorium, I knew I'd be there.

The service was to begin at two o'clock, but friends warned that I didn't stand a chance of getting in unless I went hours earlier. I packed a sandwich and a folding stool and went to the auditorium at nine o'clock. Already the lobby was filled and a hundred or so persons spilled out onto the sidewalk. The Holy Spirit was in evidence as clusters of people sang "Oh! How I Love Jesus!" and other familiar songs, while other groups prayed. The crush was so great that several persons fainted – a phenomenon which seemed contradictory for a healing service.

At one, when the doors opened, people poured through like thirsty cows stampeding for the river in those western movies. In no time, the 20,000 seats were filled. Fortunately, my strategy for getting a seat had worked, and I was where I had intended to be – in the balcony with a view of the whole scene.

In a roped-off section, there were hundreds of persons in wheel chairs and on stretchers. My heart was filled with compassion and wonder. Would these people go away healed, or disillusioned?

The house lights dimmed, and the organ burst forth with "How Great Thou Art!" When the curtain was drawn, there stood Miss Kuhlman, looking like an angel. Her long auburn hair shone like silk and her long chiffon dress was like driven snow. Holding out her arms as if to embrace the thousands of persons, she shouted, "God loves you!" Then she brought a message entitled "With God, All Things Are Possible," stressing that God's power to heal exceeds the power of man and nature. "I say *God's* power," she reiterated, "not Kathryn Kuhlman's."

Then the healing portion of the service began. "I can feel the presence of the Holy Spirit moving in — he is moving in on the lady in the left balcony — the one wearing the steel brace. The Lord is healing you right this minute. Take off that brace and bring it to me on this stage. . . . The man in the left aisle — you are being healed of cancer. Come up here on the stage with me. . . ."

This went on for hours. The stage remained filled with people. Some fell onto the floor when Miss Kuhlman touched them and the Holy Spirit moved into their lives. I wanted to see even greater miracles performed, and I didn't have long to wait. A six-year-old boy, crippled from polio and wearing two leg braces (one with a built-up shoe), was brought up in his wheel chair. Miss Kuhlman placed her hands on the lad and said, "In the name of Jesus Christ, walk to me." He got out of the chair, steadied himself a moment, then walked to her. At her urging, his parents took off his braces and he ran back and forth across the stage. I had seen an astounding demonstration of God's power!

Strangely, some were not healed. Why? What was missing?

In an attempt to learn everything I could about the Holy Spirit, I searched the scriptures and read tracts and other literature. I also went to a "believer's meeting" at a church on Peachtree Street.

The throng was already singing when I entered, and I joined in. Suddenly, everyone stood, reaching their upturned palms high into the air. A gray-haired gentleman directly in front of me began praising Jesus, and suddenly he lapsed into a language that I didn't understand. I felt ill at ease. To keep from being conspicuous, I turned my palms upward, but I didn't raise my hands very high.

As I rode home, I tried to reconcile my positive and negative feelings. On the one hand, I admired the seeming sincerity and genuineness of these people; on the other, I found myself still doubting — certainly, I had been reluctant to proclaim my Savior in this way. During the next few weeks, I prayed more earnestly than ever before, but invariably my path to God became clogged with doubts and fears or petty digressions.

One day, I described my feelings of despair to a friend, who suggested that I attend her church, Mount Paran Church of God, and hear Dr. Paul Walker. I did, and I was so intrigued that I arranged to meet him for counseling.

Frankly, I was disappointed with our first session. I expected him to lay his hands upon me right off, whereupon I would immediately receive the gift of the Holy Spirit. Instead, he talked with me, gave me some books, and arranged an appointment for a young couple — Jim Tumlin and his wife, Malone — to counsel with me.

By the time of the appointment, I had digested the materials Dr. Walker had given me. Again, I became impatient as my new friends explained to me the nature of the Holy Spirit and the demands for faith by which he is received. They emphasized that I had to relinquish control over my will and place myself in God's hands. I had to cleanse myself of all doubt before I could approach God and ask his gift.

Finally, Jim and Malone placed their hands upon me and the three of us lifted our voices in prayer. I felt a deep sense of God's power at work in my heart. I knew that I had received the gift of the Holy Spirit and was overjoyed when I heard myself speaking in a new heavenly language — a sign which reassured me that I had been baptized in the Spirit. I now use this heavenly language in my private devotions as I communicate with God through my very own, personal, direct channel.

I consider the date of this baptism — February 10, 1973 — my new birthday, for at this time I became a new person.

Several months after this conversion experience, I discovered another lump in my right breast. The doctor diagnosed my problem as an egg-sized tumor with a smaller tumor attached. I went into the hospital for my twelfth round of major surgery.

At my request, Jim and Malone came to my room the night before my surgery. Jim read aloud James 5:14-15: "Is anyone sick? He should call for the elders of the church and they should pray over him and pour a little oil upon him, calling on the Lord to heal him. And their prayer, if offered in faith, will heal him, for the Lord will make him well; and if his sickness was caused by some sin, the Lord will forgive him."

Jim anointed me with oil. Then, the four of us — Jim, Malone, Ollie, and I — held hands and prayed for my healing. The Holy Spirit came into the room and I felt electrified.

I said goodnight to our friends, and Ollie walked down the hall with them. Left to myself, I felt for the tumors.

"They're gone! They're gone!" I shouted as Ollie came through the door. He, too, was unable to detect the lumps. He knelt at my bed and together we praised the Lord, praying until we heard a second call that visiting hours were over.

The next morning, a nurse came in to give me a hypodermic. I told her I had been healed and didn't need surgery.

"I really have no choice but to give you this sedative," she said. "Talk with the doctor when he comes."

By the time the doctor arrived, I was groggy and my tongue was thick. He popped his head in the door and said, "How's my patient this morning?"

I attempted to tell him about my healing, but I guess I didn't make much sense.

"You just relax," he said. "I'll see you downstairs in a couple of minutes."

I went to surgery. On awakening, I was filled with my old apprehensions of a radical mastectomy. I clutched my bosom and once again was filled with joy not to have lost a breast.

The doctor explained that he had done an exploratory operation. "Sometimes these things just go away" was all he would say.

This healing experience brought new zest into my life. I felt less anxious; I made decisions with greater confidence. I wanted to tell the world of my wonderful experiences — and I made a good start. I changed jobs and had more time to serve the Lord and his church.

Then, in the wee hours of Sunday, September 9, 1973, I woke up with my chest paining me as though a truck were parked on it. I couldn't breathe. Fingers of fire reached into my left arm and up into my neck.

I rolled myself off the bed and writhed on the floor. Meanwhile, Ollie summoned an ambulance from our county fire department. Soon a well-trained rescue unit arrived and whisked me to the hospital. I was placed in intensive care, where it soon was confirmed that I had suffered a heart attack.

I was in the intensive care unit for a week, followed by two additional weeks of intermediate care. During this time I felt that the lights in my new and wonderful world had been extinguished just when they were burning more gloriously than ever before. I tried to cling to my faith, yet I couldn't resist asking, "Why, Lord? Why now?"

It grieved me that I had so soon suffered a spiritual relapse, but then I remembered I was only a babe — nine months old — for that's how much time had elapsed since I became a new person through my baptism of the Spirit. For fifty years, God had been trying to get me to become patient. God wasn't about to give up on me now, and knowing this contributed greatly to my peace of mind and my physical recovery. God heals! I know he does!

21

a love story

Twenty-five years after I married Ollie on impulse (he dared me, you'll remember), I fell in love with this wonderful guy. That was ten years ago. Now, looking back, the delay seems improbable – and dreadfully wasteful. But then, I'm certain that some people marry and *never* fall in love.

I'm sure that right from the start I wanted to love Ollie, and Ollie wanted to love me, but there were always walls between us. First, there was my striving nature. I had suffered the ravages of harsh poverty. I nursed a wounded ego, and people were forever pouring salt into the wound. Also, I had an insatiable craving for fame. I set unreasonable goals, and often I raised them if I was about to reach them. Worst, I wanted to be wanted but found myself unable to give or receive.

Our personalities were so different. I was volatile, spontaneous, demonstrable. I laughed, cried, or flared at the slightest provocation. Ollie, on the other hand, was quiet, dependable, and an admirer of convention and tradition. He wanted to be man of the house, the provider, and he couldn't tolerate my ambition to win riches and put us on easy street. He couldn't understand how a wife and mother could abandon her family to pursue a dream. Deep down, I couldn't accept this behavior, either; consequently, I was ridden with guilt. In moments when I should have been totally invested in my husband, my mind wandered. I began charting my next step toward becoming somebody, or I began experiencing feelings of worthlessness for having failed at the last step.

We fell in love in the empty-nest stage — the stage when statistics say so many couples fall out of love. But our romance didn't begin to glow because our children had grown up, married, and moved out — it happened because, praise God, Jesus moved in, filling the vacancy in our home and hearts.

As we learned to pray together, we learned to be open and honest with each other. I believe that if a man and wife can share a prayer life, they can share any other aspect of life. There is good therapy in doing things together, and I especially recommend sharing devotionals, spiritual outreach, and church and community activities. For so many years, I focused my attention on a dramatic career, and since I felt Ollie had nothing to offer in this regard, I shut him out. Likewise, he immersed himself in his business affairs — mostly because he loved his career, but also because it compensated for a lack of zest in our marriage.

When Jesus came in, the walls separating us came tumbling down. Our inhibitions and taboos melted, enabling us to come together in a joyous union of body and spirit. Our defensiveness evaporated. We were able to laugh at ourselves and with each other.

Our life-style has changed radically. Oh, I still like gaiety, music, dancing, bright conversation, new and exciting people — but I'm strangely content for us to spend most of our evenings quietly at home together.

I remember the first Christmas that was different. Until then, the Jordans' party was *the* social event in Glendale. People were hurt if they didn't make the guest list, and we were hurt if the party wasn't talked about for months.

"Ollie, let's not have a Christmas party this year."

"No Christmas party?"

"I've never been more serious. I've suddenly recognized

that our parties leave Christ out. It's like — well, like having a birthday party for Gayle and not inviting her to come."

That year, we attended someone else's extravaganza. At eleven, we slipped away and drove to the church. We knelt at the altar, just the two of us, waiting for the Baby Jesus to come again. And he did come. He came into our hearts and we took him home with us.

New Year's Eve found us in the church again. Outside there was a bedlam of horns, sirens, and firecrackers, but in our hearts there was the quiet of God's presence. He helped us prepare ourselves for the coming year.

I especially cherish one new dimension in our lives — tenderness. Early in our married life, Ollie and I weren't capable of tenderness. Oh, Ollie sometimes was, but I was too self-centered.

Let me draw you a picture of tenderness:

Ollie wakes me with a kiss and a cup of coffee — and I know I'm crazy about him.

He comes in evenings and calls, "Baby, I'm home!" — and my heart and feet race to him.

He's promoted to vice president of his company — and I'm proud of him, not because I've become the wife of a vice president (my old system of values), but because it means a lot to Ollie as a person.

I step on the bathroom scales — and I'm gratified to see the pointer stop where I want it to stop, because Ollie will notice and care.

At a social function, he whispers in my ear that I'm the most beautiful woman there — and I no longer fret over whether or not it's really true.

To fall in love at middle age is especially wonderful because that's when you need love most. Being in love can make you beautiful (or handsome), put sparkle in your eye, liveliness in your step, a lilt in your voice. It keeps you buying red nightgowns, singing love songs, building dream castles.

We've begun living as never before. Why? Because the Lord is at work in our lives. I've learned that when you write down what the Lord has done for you, you've written a love story. Middle age is a time for reflection and summing up. As I sum things up I have reasons for rejoicing.

My daddy has succeeded in fulfilling his own dream of becoming somebody — he's thrown off the shackles of share-cropping. He now owns his own home and farmlands and is considered well-to-do. Mother, who has helped him to realize this ambition, can relish knowing that she did a good job rearing us kids, who were at the center of her life.

Six of us children are living and doing well. Earl, who shared so many of my young misadventures, is an electrical contractor. My four sisters are happily married and are, like Earl, making their own contributions to the world.

Our own children have given us much joy. Gayle has her master's degree and teaches science. She and her husband, Jim Doran, an insurance executive, have two children, Chris and Stacey. Sandy is a homemaker, wrapped up in her cooking, canning, and gardening. Her husband, Uel Gardner, is a professional ski instructor. You ought to see their sons, Mark and Uel Jordan, on the slopes! And Leonard, who married Monique, a French girl, is a businessman in Arizona. They're the parents of Mike, my oldest grandson.

Middle age is a time for reflection, but also a time for anticipation. I expect to have enough new adventures to fill another book.

As I have said, I'm only an infant in terms of the recency of my baptism by the Holy Spirit, so I have a lot of growing yet to do. I look forward to learning more about the Christian life and witness. And I'm keenly aware that, living in a vibrant metropolis as I do, there are unlimited possibilities for service.

My twelve major operations and recent heart attack have taught me some things about life and living that would otherwise have escaped me. I wouldn't wish the emotional crises and dreadful suffering on anybody; still, they are a part of my experience and I can share them with others. I believe that each chapter of our lives has its ultimate purpose

— a twofold purpose: to know ourselves so that we can grow personally, and to understand other people so that we can help them in their situations.

I thank God for reaching out to touch the seemingly barren and hopeless life of a young girl in a south Georgia cotton patch. I thank him for the softness of a Papa Leslie and the fiery urgings of an Aunt Mary. I thank him for placing me in a home where a father and mother tried to do their best for their children. I'm thankful for Ollie, for my daughters, and for my son — a son that only God could have given me. I also thank God for all those unexpected somebodies (so varied in color, station, education, and experience) whom he sent into my life at precisely the right time.

From the start, God has had plans for my life. Rather early, I sensed that he wanted me to be somebody; however, my vanity and drive distorted the picture. Now I have moved out from under the sign of the Ram and am under the sign of the Cross. Now I know that I have to listen, to be submissive, to give God room in which to operate. I have to be open to each opportunity for personal growth and social service.

God had made me a somebody even before I came into the loving, experienced hands of Nar Sis, the midwife. I was somebody from the start, but it has taken me a lifetime to recognize my identity and destiny, which continue to unfold each day. I feel that God meant for it to be this way. If I had found myself to be a full-blown somebody right off, how could I now relate to those who are commencing their journey toward accepting their own personhood?

The title of my book is *Someday I'll Be Somebody*. It is a very personal story, and I have tried to be open and honest in the telling of it. The word "I" has appeared many, many times. Throughout the writing, however, *you* have been on my mind.

Open up every aspect of your life to God; learn what kind of somebody he wants you to be. One of my favorite verses is, "Taste and see that the Lord is good." (Psalms 34:8) The

Lord *is* good, but you have to come near enough to taste his goodness. You have to relinquish your self-will and surrender to his will. This may suggest a fearsome loss of personhood, but it is not. As you walk with God along life's way, conversing with him about even the smallest details of your life, you will see a glorious dawn breaking. Your nightmares will become sweet dreams. As you approach each fork in the road, he will be there helping you to choose the right — the most fulfilling — path.

For half a century, God has been telling me, "Someday you'll be somebody." Only recently have I come to understand that by "someday" he meant *today*. I am somebody today — and you are somebody. God loves you. Praise the Lord!

I wish to thank
my friends (too numerous to name)
for their inspiration, prayers, and other contributions
to my life
and to this book.

MICKEY JORDAN

DATE DUE

MAR 9 '83			
MAY 9 '83			